ANTICHRIST

Invades Earth

OUR FUTURE

Thomas Velez

To Ramon,

God Bless you + give you understanding as you read this!

Thomas Vel

INTRODUCTION

My previous book, "Understanding the Book of Revelation", was a verse-by-verse commentary or interpretation of the entire Book of Revelation, in the same order and with the same numbering of chapters and verses as is presented in the Holy Bible. Included with the plain English explanations were multitudes of applicable Bible verses, gathered from throughout the Bible that corroborated and enhanced the understanding of the verses being explained. Along with schedules, a Glossary of definitions and cross-references was provided to help the reader understand the Biblical terms used in the Book of Revelation and to understand what or who they meant and the significance of each, with alternate names, etc. for the same. That Glossary is also included as an Appendix to this book. That earlier book was an easy reading reference book, in the original Biblical sequence, which in many cases became a series of short stories based on the many separate visions that the Apostle John received from which he wrote the Book of Revelation.

This new book is a narrative chronological story, explaining the coming future events in the order in which they actually will happen, including a great satanic deception before Jesus Christ returns to the Earth.

2 Thes 2:11 *And for this cause God shall send them strong delusion* (DECEPTION), *that they should believe a lie:*

2 Thes 2:12 *That they all might be damned who believed not the truth, but had pleasure in unrighteousness.*

This book clearly tells the story of what that deception is and how it comes to pass. This book is based on the Biblical interpretations presented in my previous book "Understanding the Book of Revelation" as well as new subsequent revelation given to me by God's Holy Spirit, which I have received since publishing my previous book. There are no contradictions, but much has been added to clearly identify and expose the great deception that is coming upon the Earth. People who do not recognize this deception when it comes will be in very serious spiritual trouble. I pray that this does not catch you in the snare of being unaware! (Luke 21:35)

Additionally, as an Appendix to this book, a scripture study is presented which provides an alternative interpretation to many of the scriptures commonly used to claim a pre-tribulation rapture of the Church. Please examine these closely.

To God and Jesus Christ and the Holy Spirit be all the glory!

TABLE OF CONTENTS

Tables & Charts

CHAPTER ONE

The Evolution of the Church until Now

Since the birth, death, burial, and resurrection of God's only begotten Son, Jesus Christ, His Church has evolved through the ages. The foundation of the Church is built upon the Apostles and Prophets, Jesus Christ being the Chief Cornerstone. As the Bible says:

> Ephesians 2.:19 *Now therefore ye are no more strangers and foreigners, but fellowcitizens with the saints, and of the household of God;*
> Ephesians 2:20 *And are built upon the foundation of the apostles and prophets, Jesus Christ himself being the chief corner {stone};*

The evolution of the Church was described in the Holy Bible, in the Book of Revelation, chapters 2 and 3, which contain the letters to seven churches that actually existed during the time of John the Apostle. However, history shows that the chronological presentation of these letters in the Bible also represents how the Church has evolved over the last two thousand years. This was also described in more detail in my previous book: Understanding the Book of Revelation. However in this new book, this chapter will only briefly mention the history of the Church indicating the major periods of this church evolution until now, to set the stage for what is to quickly come upon the Earth.

After Jesus Christ, the story of the evolution of the Church began with the letter to the first church, named **EPHESUS**, written about in the Book of Revelation (abbreviated as "Rev") chapter (abbreviated as "ch"), in Rev ch 2:1-7 (chapter 2, verses 1-7). This first church period was the age of the early apostles and prophets, and continued until about 64 AD, the time of Nero, Emperor of Rome.

The second church period, began with Nero and was represented by the letter to the church of **SMYRNA**, written about in Rev 2:8-11 (lasting from approximately 64 AD to 312 AD). This was a time of great persecution and martyrdom under ten Caesars of Rome.

The third church period, was represented in the letter to the church in **PERGAMOS**, written about in Rev 2:12-17. This church period lasted from 312 AD to about 376 AD. In this time, a man named Constantine became the Caesar of Rome and stopped the persecution of Christians. He and his followers also made Christianity a state religion and over time, offered enticements to Christians leading the Church into worldliness by compromising with the State (government). (Endnote 1)

The fourth church period in the evolution of the Church was described in the letter to the church of **THYATIRA**, in Rev 2:18-29. This was also the church of the "dark ages". This was the beginning of a church hierarchy being established. A bishop of Rome gained political power from the Roman emperor, and over other churches. This was the beginning of the consolidated office of the "Pontiff", or Pope. This church taught people to pray to, and to sacrifice to, idols/statues/images claimed to represent god and people/beings in heaven. This church also insisted on such unbiblical practices as having to confess your sins to a priest instead of Jesus, purchase "indulgences" to get people out of "purgatory" earlier (a sort of extortion), and performing the sacrifice of the "Mass". The sacrifice of the Mass was and still is believed by Roman Catholics to be an actual "re-crucifixion" or re-killing of Christ, and that the sacred elements of the Holy Communion (the bread and the wine) are actually the actual physical body and blood of Jesus. This is called the doctrine of "transubstantiation" and must be believed by Catholics to obtain their salvation. This was instituted as "dogma" (a mandatory belief) by the Roman Catholic Church in 1215 AD. (Endnote 2) This changing of the earthly elements into the actual body and blood of Jesus is believed to be accomplished by the power vested in a Catholic priest. The communion wafer is then eaten.

In the Book of Revelation 2:21-22, Jesus said that since this church would not repent (verse 21), this church with its followers, will be taken into great tribulation (before the Second Coming of Jesus Christ). This means that this Roman Catholic Church will remain on Earth, in a state of power, until and into the great tribulation before Jesus' Second Coming. It will not fade or pass away before then, as previous churches had. More details about this Roman Catholic Church, the Vatican and the Pope will be explained in the next chapter.

The fifth church period is covered in the Book of Revelation, chapter 3, verses 1-6, in the letter to the church of **SARDIS**. This represented the early protestant movement church age, beginning in the early 16th century. Christ says He knows the works of the people of this church. He knows how they name the name of Christ (are called Christians), but are really dead (having degenerated into a deadness, no life - no fervent love-asleep - no enthusiasm for Christ - lazy - indifferent). Most did not believe in the need for, or necessarily practice, personal holiness in their lives. This church age also continues until Jesus' Second Coming, partially being blended later into the Church of Laodicea, yet to be explained.

The sixth church period was described in the letter to the Church of **PHILADELPHIA**, Rev 3:7-14. This was a church age of personal holiness, lasting from about 1750 AD until approximately 1950 AD. Most of these people lived in the United States. This personal holiness lifestyle occurred during the founding times of such church movements such as the Baptists and Methodists and Pentecostals. These people believed that they also had to live a holy life as well as have faith in Jesus.

In Revelation 3:10, Jesus explained that because these have patiently obeyed His word, this church age shall pass away before the "hour of temptation" comes, which shall come upon all the world, just before Jesus'

Second Coming. This hour of temptation will come upon all the world after most people stop believing in and practicing personal holiness. This hour of temptation will be to try the people of this world at that time, forcing them to make a choice. More details on this are explained in the notes for the next Church phase (Laodicea).

The seventh church period was described in the letter to the church of **LAODICEA**, Rev 3:14-22. This is the lukewarm church that we now find ourselves living in. This church and its ways are totally rejected by Jesus. Jesus does not approve of anyone being lukewarm in their relationship with Him. Since we are now living in this Laodicean church period, I have taken the liberty to copy and present here the explanation of this portion of the Book of Revelation, as recorded in my book "Understanding the Book of Revelation". The initial numbers below refer to the corresponding chapter and verse in the Book of Revelation in the Holy Bible. You may wish to consult your Bible and read the actual Biblical verses along with their explanation below.

"3:14   To the church of LAODICEA, formerly, a rich city in the valley of Lycus near Colosse and Hierapolis. (Endnote 3) It is now uninhabited. This church represents the church age after the age of personal holiness. This begins about the mid-twentieth century (from about 1950 AD). This age continues until Christ's second coming. Christ - the Faithful and true Witness - says:

3:15   I know your works. You are not fervently cold in attitude (towards the Lord), neither are you fervently hot (for the Lord). You are lukewarm (the word is in Strong's Concordance, word #5513, meaning lukewarm or wretchedly fluctuating between torpor-inactivity, sluggishness, or stagnation-and a fervor of love). Christ wishes they were either fervently against or for Him.

3:16   Since they are lukewarm - refusing to choose, refusing to be separated from the world, refusing to take a stand for Jesus Christ, - Christ spues them out of His mouth, He totally REJECTS them! (Strong's Concordance #1692 for spue, means to vomit.) Christ came to cause a separation between His followers and the world -Matt 10:34-39 and James 4:4. Also remember Elijah's famous words in 1 Kings 18:21, "How long halt ye between two opinions?"

Matthew 10:34 *Think not that I am come to send peace on earth: I came not to send peace, but a sword.*
Matthew 10:35 *For I am come to set a man at variance against his father, and the daughter against her mother, and the daughter in law against her mother in law.*
Matthew 10:36 *And a man's foes {shall be} they of his own household.*
Matthew 10:37 *He that loveth father or mother more than me is not worthy of me: and he that loveth son or daughter more than me is not worthy of me.*
Matthew 10:38 *And he that taketh not his cross, and followeth after me, is not worthy of me.*
Matthew 10:39 *He that findeth his life shall lose it: and he that loseth his life for my sake shall find it.*

James 4:4 *Ye adulterers and adulteresses, know ye not that the friendship of the world is enmity with God? whosoever therefore will be a friend of the world is the enemy of God.*

1 Kings 18:21 *And Elijah came unto all the people, and said, How long halt ye between two opinions? if the LORD {be} God, follow him: but if Baal, {then} follow him. And the people answered him not a word.*

3:17   Because you say you are rich (Strong's Concordance #4145: wealthy, abundantly supplied) and you don't know your true condition (the deceitfulness of riches -Mark 4:19) that you are really:

Mark 4:19 *And the cares of this world, and the deceitfulness of riches, and the lusts of other things entering in, choke the word, and it becometh unfruitful.*

    a. wretched - Strong's Concordance # 5005 and Webster's Dictionary: afflicted, nearly worthless, inferior, of very poor quality or ability
    b. miserable - unhappy - Strong's Concordance # 1652: to be pitied, miserable
    c. poor - spiritually. Strong's Concordance # 4434: destitute of wealth, influence, position, honor, lowly, and destitute of Christian virtues and eternal riches.
    d. blind - spiritually. Strong's Concordance # 5185, to be blind, or mentally blind
    e. naked - sins showing because they are not washed by the blood of Jesus Christ or covered with His righteousness. Strong's Concordance # 1131: to be unclothed, or metaphorically to be open or laid bare.

3:18   The Lord says buy from Him

a.   gold tried in the fire (Strong's Concordance #4448; tried means to be burned by the fire and purged of dross) that you may be rich (Strong's Concordance #4147, to have abundance).

Allow the Lord to teach you and lead you through fiery trials to refine you - to remove the impurities from your life - that YOU may become that gold tried in the fire (1 Pe 4:12)-that you may be truly rich (spiritually rich). See Mark 9: 49, every one shall be salted with fire. Is 48:10 says God chooses us in the furnace of affliction.

> 1 Peter 4:12 *Beloved, think it not strange concerning the fiery trial which is to try you, as though some strange thing happened unto you:*

> Mark 9:49 *For every one shall be salted with fire, and every sacrifice shall be salted with salt.*

> Isaiah 48:10 *Behold, I have refined thee, but not with silver; I have chosen thee in the furnace of affliction.*

b.   white (Strong's Concordance #3022, light, bright, brilliant, as of heavenly angels) garments (Strong's Concordance # 2440, vesture), that you be clothed and that the shame (Strong's Concordance #152 , shame, disgrace, dishonour) of your nakedness (Strong's Concordance #1132, nakedness) does not appear (Strong's Concordance # 5319 be made known).

We need to procure from the Lord, the brilliant covering garment of the heavenly. This is the covering garment that has been made available to us by the blood of Jesus Christ. This is the righteousness of Christ, by having your sins forgiven by Christ that your sins do not show.

c.   anoint your eyes with eyesalve (Strong's Concordance #2854, a mixture for tender eyelids), that you may see (Strong's Concordance #991, to see, perceive, understand, discover by use, know by experience, discern mentally).

Read Matt 6:21-23, be single minded for God. E.g.; read the Bible and let it teach you. "Faith cometh by hearing (understanding), and hearing (understanding) by the the Word of God-Romans 10:17. Anoint your eyes that you might not be blinded by Satan (2 Cor 4:4), that you might see (understand) the glorious gospel of Christ.

Matthew 6:21 *For where your treasure is, there will your heart be also.*
Matthew 6:22 *The light of the body is the eye: if therefore thine eye be single, thy whole body shall be full of light.*
Matthew 6:23 *But if thine eye be evil, thy whole body shall be full of darkness. If therefore the light that is in thee be darkness, how great {is} that darkness!*

Romans 10:17 *So then faith {cometh} by hearing, and hearing by the word of God.*

2 Corinthians 4:4 *In whom the god of this world hath blinded the minds of them which believe not, lest the light of the glorious gospel of Christ, who is the image of God, should shine unto them.*

3:19   As many as the Lord loves, He will rebuke and chasten (discipline in an attempt to teach obedience). Be zealous (fervent, eager) and change!

3:20   Christ stands at the door of your heart, knocking, wanting to come in (for your eternal benefit). If anyone hears and opens their heart to Jesus, He will come into that person and will dwell with him. If you have not already done so, ask Jesus into your heart, and He will live within you, and guide you unto an eternal life with Him in Heaven.

3:21   They that overcome will sit with Christ in His throne in the temple; even as Christ overcame the world by His death. Many of this church age (today) will overcome the world by their martyrdom, even as Christ also overcame the world. Christ paid the ultimate price of loyalty to God. Many today and in the future will also pay the ultimate price of loyalty to Christ.

3:22   Hear, understand, and obey, what the Spirit of God is saying as recorded by John."

Many true movements of God have occurred throughout church history. However, many later have been turned into lifeless religious remnants, usually by replacing the leadership and spontaneity of the Holy Spirit with the institutionalizing of traditions or by imposing a hierarchy of leadership. The idea is that devils want to control the people and keep them from freely following the Holy Spirit of God. All true religious movements of God believe in and agree that the initial act of the salvation of one's soul is <u>only</u> by: repentance to and acceptance of the only begotten Son of God, Jesus Christ, who was:

     a. Fathered by God
     b. born of a virgin
     c. born in the flesh
     d. lived a sinless life
     e. died once for our sins
     f. was resurrected
     g. and is alive today and forevermore.

Only Jesus can forgive sins: not any man. No man is to be a mediator between God and us-only Jesus.

1 Tim 2:5 *For there is one God, and one mediator between God and men, the man Christ Jesus;*
1 Tim 2:6 *Who gave himself a ransom for all, to be testified in due time.*

Jesus paid the price for our salvation. This salvation affects every area of a Christian's life. However, the most important part of salvation is having our sins forgiven, enabling us to be with Jesus and God forever, and not having to be eternally punished in the lake of fire with the devil and his followers.

Scripture says:

Rom 3:10 *As it is written, There is none righteous, no, not one:*

Rom 6:23 *For the wages of sin is death; but the gift of God is eternal life through Jesus Christ our Lord.*

Rom 10:9 *That if thou shalt confess with thy mouth the Lord Jesus, and shalt believe in thine heart that God hath raised him from the dead, thou shalt be saved.*
Rom 10:10 *For with the heart man believeth unto righteousness; and with the mouth confession is made unto salvation.*

If you have not done it yet, admit to Jesus that you have sinned and ask Jesus to forgive you for your past life and ask Him to come and live within you and be your Lord (boss). You will find more than you ever hoped for, and you will have a best friend for life, that will never leave you or forsake you, no matter what the circumstances. Do not feel that you are not worthy. No one is worthy, but Jesus died for us anyway, while we were yet sinners, because we were all sinners. This salvation through Jesus is a free gift. We cannot earn it, and we do not have to wait until we first get our life cleaned up. Jesus wants us to come to Him as we are, now, and He will help us. You will find that you will have a new power from within, to help you overcome your sinful habits, and with Jesus you will have a peace within that lifts you above the circumstances of your life and He can even lead you in what you should do in every circumstance. This is priceless.

Evolution of the Church-Schedule: Revelation Ch 2 & 3
(Not to Scale & Dates are Approximate)

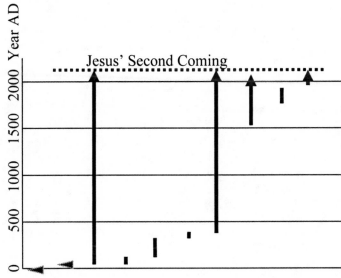

Jesus Born-Rev chapter 12:5

Book of Revelation Written-Rev chapter 1

Time of Evolution of Churches-Rev ch 2 & 3

Ephesus: Rev ch 2:1-7 (to 64 AD)

Smyrna: Rev 2:8-11 (64 AD to 312 AD)

Pergamos: Rev 2:12-17 (312 AD to 376 AD)

Thyatira: Rev 2:18-29 (378 AD to Jesus 2nd Coming)

Sardis: Rev 3:1-6 (beginning early1500s)

Philadelphia: Rev 3:7-13 (mid 1700s to mid 1900s)

Laodicia: Rev 3:14-22 (mid 1900s to Jesus 2nd Coming)

Thomas Velez

CHAPTER TWO

The Vatican
and
The Rise of the False Prophet

To better understand the Vatican, Rome, and the Roman Catholic Church, it is helpful to review a little of its history. The Microsoft Encarta Encyclopedia Standard 2004, (Endnote 4) in the article entitled "Papal States" says:

"Papal States, territory of Italy formerly under direct temporal rule of the pope. They were also known as the States of the Church or Pontifical States. The popes became de facto rulers of the city of Rome and the surrounding area by the 6th century ad. This territory was formally granted to Pope Stephen II by Pepin the Short, king of the Franks, in 754. Additions were made by gifts, purchases, and conquests until the Papal States included nearly the whole of central Italy, reaching their greatest extent in the 16th century. The acquisitions of the papacy were for the most part retained until 1797, when French forces under Napoleon Bonaparte seized much of the territory. In 1801 Pope Pius VII regained some power, and in 1815 the Congress of Vienna restored nearly all the territory of the states, placing them under Austrian protection.

The final dissolution of the Papal States came in 1870, when nearly all the territory, including Rome, was annexed to a united Italy by its king, Victor Emmanuel II. The jurisdiction of the pope was confined to the Vatican, in which, as a protest against the Italian occupation, each succeeding pope remained a voluntary prisoner until 1929, when the Lateran Treaty recognized the full and independent sovereignty of the Holy See in Vatican City."

Additionally, the Microsoft Encarta Encyclopedia Standard 2004, © 1993-2003 Microsoft Corporation, in the separate article entitled "Vatican City", says:

"Vatican City, independent state, under the absolute authority of the pope of the Roman Catholic church. It is an enclave within Rome, Italy, with an area of 44 hectares (110 acres). The smallest independent country in the world, Vatican City was established in 1929 under terms of the Lateran Treaty, concluded by the Italian government and the papacy after many years of controversy."

In 1929, the city of the Vatican became a separate, independent, country, with full privileges of statehood. The Vatican has ambassadors to the United Nations and to the United States, as do other sovereign countries. The Vatican is located in Rome, Italy.

Rev ch 17 of the Book of Revelation tells the end time story of what, in verse 5, is called "Mystery, Babylon the Great, the Mother of Harlots and Abominations of the Earth".

Rev 17:5 *And upon her forehead was a name written, MYSTERY, BABYLON THE GREAT, THE MOTHER OF HARLOTS AND ABOMINATIONS OF THE EARTH.*

It is situated at seven mountains or hills (verse 9).

Rev 17:9 *And here is the mind which hath wisdom. The seven heads are seven mountains, on which the woman sitteth.*

Verse 18 more clearly identifies this woman, known as "Mystery, Babylon the Great", that sits on the seven mountains as a city.

Rev 17:18 *And the woman which thou sawest is that great city, which reigneth over the kings of the earth.*

The Vatican is a city/state/country and the headquarters of a Church and is located in Rome, Italy. Rome is known as the city of seven hills. These seven heads (Rev 17:9) are the seven mountains or hills of Rome, on which the woman sits. "The seven hills on which Rome was built are: the Palatine Hill, the Capitoline Hill, the Quirinal Hill, the Aventine Hill, the Caelian Hill, the Esquiline Hill, and the Viminal Hill". (Endnote 5)

In John's time, Rome was the center or capital of the political and military power of the Roman empire. Today the center or capital of this "Mystery Babylon" empire is the Vatican, in Rome. This is the headquarters of the Roman Catholic Church/empire. This is the first and only reason for the Vatican's existence, to rule over the Roman Catholic Church/empire, and the head of the Roman Catholic Church, the Pope, has absolute power over this city/country/empire. The empire and influence of the Roman Catholic Church extends far beyond its geographic borders and has influenced the rise and fall of rulers and peoples for hundreds of years, as witnessed by the history of Europe, South America, the Middle Eastern Crusades, etc.

God hates the leadership and idolatry of this false Church, the Roman Catholic Church. This is what will happen later, but it is presented here to demonstrate which way the Roman Catholic Church will go, and God's attitude toward it.

Rev 18:1 *And after these things I saw another angel come down from heaven, having great power; and the earth was lightened with his glory.*

Rev 18:2 And he cried mightily with a strong voice, saying, Babylon the great is fallen, is fallen, and is become the habitation of devils, and the hold of every foul spirit, and a cage of every unclean and hateful bird.

Rev 18:3 For all nations have drunk of the wine of the wrath of her fornication, and the kings of the earth have committed fornication with her, and the merchants of the earth are waxed rich through the abundance of her delicacies.

Rev 18:4 And I heard another voice from heaven, saying, Come out of her, my people, that ye be not partakers of her sins, and that ye receive not of her plagues.

Rev 18:5 For her sins have reached unto heaven, and God hath remembered her iniquities.

Note: It is important to remember, that God does not hate the individual people of this false Church, but calls some of them His people (verse 4) and calls for them to come out of this false Church, that they not be considered a partaker of the sins and punishments of this false Church, because judgment is coming.

Each Pope is actually like a King of the country of the Vatican. They are elected by the College of Cardinals and they serve for life. The reason that they are elected, unlike most kings, is because they are not supposed to be married or have children, thus they leave no heir to the throne, and therefore the next successor must be elected by those in power.

In Rev 17:9-10, it explains that there are seven kings of this city/state/country/headquarters/empire.

Rev 17:9 And here is the mind which hath wisdom. The seven heads are seven mountains, on which the woman sitteth.

Rev 17:10 And there are seven kings: five are fallen, and one is, and the other is not yet come; and when he cometh, he must continue a short space.

As I wrote in my previous book "Understanding the Book of Revelation", which was first published in early 2005, in the explanation for 17:10:

"And the seven heads are seven kings. The Treaty of Conciliation (Feb 11, 1929) established the Vatican as an independent country. At the time of this writing, in the year 2002, the kings of the country of Vatican were and are:

1st = Pius 11th = fallen, deceased
2nd = Pius 12th = fallen, deceased
3rd = John 23rd = fallen, deceased
4th = Paul 6th = fallen, deceased
5th = John Paul 1st = fallen, deceased
6th = John Paul 2nd = alive at the reference time of verse 10, (and alive now [in 2002])
Note: This head, John Paul 2, suffered a deadly wound in an assignation attempt at the Vatican in May of 1981. He fully recovered. This is the deadly wound to the head/king described in Rev 13:3.
7th= is not yet come; and when he cometh, he must continue a short space.
This is the next Pope. This is the one who will be Pope after John Paul 2. This is the Pope who will side with the Antichrist when he comes in person among mankind. This is the Pope into which an evil spirit known as the False Prophet will enter. (see Rev 13:11-18 and notes)."

However, we now know that this Seventh Pope/King of the country of the Vatican is now alive and serving and reigning as the new Pope/King. He is Pope Benedict the 16th. This Pope is the one who will become the False Prophet. This Pope will become the False Prophet by accepting and endorsing the Antichrist when he (the Antichrist) arrives on the scene. The Antichrist will claim to be Jesus Christ, and the Pope will accept him as the

Christ (Messiah) and encourage his Church members, the Jews, and everyone to accept him as the Christ/Messiah. More. details on this will be explained in the following chapters. Note, that since the Antichrist will come in this Pope's lifetime, and because this Pope was seventy eight years old when he was elected Pope in 2005, and since most people do not live much beyond ninety years old, there cannot be many more years left before the Antichrist arises among mankind to take control of both the Roman Catholic Church and the Earth. Also, Rev 19:20 shows that the beast (Antichrist) and the False Prophet will both be cast alive into the lake of fire, after Jesus' triumphant return to the Earth. Therefore, Jesus' Second Coming, in power and in glory, will also happen in this Pope's lifetime.

> Rev 19:19 *And I saw the beast, and the kings of the earth, and their armies, gathered together to make war against him that sat on the horse, and against his army.*
> Rev 19:20 *And the beast was taken, and with him the false prophet that wrought miracles before him, with which he deceived them that had received the mark of the beast, and them that worshipped his image. These both were <u>cast alive</u> into a lake of fire burning with brimstone.*

CHAPTER THREE

The Two Witnesses
and
The First Four Trumpets

One thing will happen very soon. The servants of God-the two witnesses-the Apostles and Prophets, will be sealed by the angels of God. This story is told in Rev chapter 7. My previous book, "Understanding the Book of Revelation" describes this more fully, but a little will be explained here, excerpted from my notes for Rev 7:4:

"John hears the number of them which were sealed; 144,000. These people all have the gift of the Holy Spirit and are born again, Spirit-filled Christians. They may be living anywhere in the world now. George Eldon Ladd, in his book, *A THEOLOGY OF THE NEW TESTAMENT*, makes a very astute point (Endnote 6):

'these twelve tribes cannot be literal Israel, because they are not the twelve tribes of Old Testament Israel. The tribes here listed nowhere appear in the entire Bible. Three irregularities appear that make it difficult if not impossible to see in these sealed ones literal Israel. Judah is named first, and thus the Old Testament order of the tribes is ignored. Dan is omitted with no explanation whatsoever. Furthermore, Joseph is mentioned instead of Ephraim.

These two facts suggest that John means by this deliberate irregular listing of the twelve tribes to designate the Israel that is not the literal Israel.

That John conceives of a spiritual Israel is shown by other references. Twice he speaks of those "who say that they are Jews and are not, but are of synagogue of Satan (2:9, 3:9). By this John means that there are people who are Jews by race but are not spiritually Jews, but are rather dupes of Satan. A real Jew, then, is not one who is racially or religiously a Jew, but one who acknowledges the claims of Christ and therefore recognizes the church as the true people of God. This the pseudo-Jews refuse to do.

With this as a clue, we may understand the twelve tribes in Revelation 7 as the true Israel, the elect of God whether Jew or Gentile.'

Therefore, we see that this 144,000 can have nothing to do with the actual Jewish race by blood, but these people may be of any race or descent. Also, the 144,000 may be a symbolic number, rather than a literal, actual, 144,000 people."

The story of the two witnesses is told in Rev chapter 11. The two witnesses are actually two groups of people. They are the called out, chosen, commissioned and faithful Apostles and Prophets of God. Ephesians 4:11-13 says that Jesus gave the fivefold ministries (apostles, prophets, evangelists, pastors, and teachers) to the church until we all come in the unity of the faith, ...". This means until Jesus comes back. Therefore, these five types of Christian ministers have been on the Earth since the time of Pentecost, until now, and until we all come in the unity of the faith-which has not happened yet.

Ephesians 4:11 *And he gave some, apostles; and some, prophets; and some, evangelists; and some, pastors and teachers;*

Ephesians 4:12 *For the perfecting of the saints, for the work of the ministry, for the edifying of the body of Christ:*
Ephesians 4:13 *Till we all come in the unity of the faith, and of the knowledge of the Son of God, unto a perfect man, unto the measure of the stature of the fulness of Christ:*

Furthermore, Ephesians 2:19-20 says the household of God is built upon the foundation of the apostles and prophets, Jesus Christ himself being the chief cornerstone.

Ephesians 2:19 *Now therefore ye are no more strangers and foreigners, but fellowcitizens with the saints, and of the household of God;*
Ephesians 2:20 *And are built upon the foundation of the apostles and prophets, Jesus Christ himself being the chief corner {stone};*

After they are sealed by the angels of God as explained above, the Apostles and Prophets will begin to declare the judgments of God upon the Earth, signified by being announced by an angel with the **FIRST TRUMPET**, described in Rev 8:7:

Rev 8:7 *The first angel sounded, and there followed hail and fire mingled with blood, and they were cast upon the earth: and the third part of trees was burnt up, and all green grass was burnt up*

The note from my previous book "Understanding the Book of Revelation" for this verse is:

Notes from 8:7 The FIRST TRUMPET is sounded. A judgment is decreed by God and announced by the two witnesses of Rev 11:3 upon the Earth. They have the power to withhold rain from the Earth-see Rev 11:6 notes. A third part of the trees, and all green grass of the spoken area are burnt up. When rain and water are withheld from grass and green vegetation, thereby lacking the water necessary for the plant process called "transpiration" they turn brown or yellow, and we say that they are "burned up".

The two witnesses shall also announce God's judgments through other forms of the weather, such as hail, storms, lightning, etc. And the notes from my previous book for Rev 11:6 are:

"These two witnesses shall have power from God to convince mankind of their sins, of impending punishment, and of the supremacy of God and His only begotten son - Jesus Christ.

Note, the supernatural powers mentioned in this verse were demonstrated in Biblical history against rulers and their followers who refused to worship and obey only God (EG: against King Ahab and Queen Jezebel, and against the Pharaoh of Egypt). Note again, that these judgments were proclaimed by prophets of God - Elijah and Moses (See 1 Kings 17:1-7, Exodus 7:19-20).

> 1 Kings 17:1 *And Elijah the Tishbite, {who was} of the inhabitants of Gilead, said unto Ahab, {As} the LORD God of Israel liveth, before whom I stand, there shall not be dew nor rain these years, but according to my word.*
> 1 Kings 17:2 *And the word of the LORD came unto him, saying,*
> 1 Kings 17:3 *Get thee hence, and turn thee eastward, and hide thyself by the brook Cherith, that {is} before Jordan.*
> 1 Kings 17:4 *And it shall be, {that} thou shalt drink of the brook; and I have commanded the ravens to feed thee there.*
> 1 Kings 17:5 *So he went and did according unto the word of the LORD: for he went and dwelt by the brook Cherith, that {is} before Jordan.*

1 Kings 17:6 *And the ravens brought him bread and flesh in the morning, and bread and flesh in the evening; and he drank of the brook.*
1 Kings 17:7 *And it came to pass after a while, that the brook dried up, because there had been no rain in the land.*

Exodus 7:19 *And the LORD spake unto Moses, Say unto Aaron, Take thy rod, and stretch out thine hand upon the waters of Egypt, upon their streams, upon their rivers, and upon their ponds, and upon all their pools of water, that they may become blood; and {that} there may be blood throughout all the land of Egypt, both in {vessels of} wood, and in {vessels of} stone.*
Exodus 7:20 *And Moses and Aaron did so, as the LORD commanded; and he lifted up the rod, and smote the waters that {were} in the river, in the sight of Pharaoh, and in the sight of his servants; and all the waters that {were} in the river were turned to blood.*

These two witnesses shall announce the judgments of God during the initial trumpets (see Rev chapter 8 notes, especially 8:7 & 8:8). These first trumpets shall be initiated during their ministry.

Amos 3:7 *Surely the Lord GOD will do nothing, but he revealeth his secret unto his servants the prophets."*

Also, Moses is an Old Testament shadow or type of the New Testament Apostle. The Greek word "apostolos" for apostle is Strongs # 652, meaning: "a delegate, messenger, one sent forth with orders". Certainly, Moses was a delegate or messenger or one sent forth with orders from God to tell Pharoah "let My people go". Moses also truly accomplished the signs of an apostle by performing many signs, wonders and mighty deeds, and proved that he had patience by interceding for his people to God. Second Corinthians in the Bible says:

2 Co 12:12 *Truly the signs of an apostle were wrought among you in all patience, in signs, and wonders, and mighty deeds.*

God will always first tell His prophets (Amos 3:7). The problem is, will people listen to them? Will they sincerely attempt to be open to the leading of the Holy Spirit to confirm or reject what is said? The Bible says in Is 55:

Is 55: 11 *So shall my word be that goeth forth out of my mouth: it shall not return unto me void, but it shall accomplish that which I please, and it shall prosper in the thing whereto I sent it.*
Is 55:12 *For ye shall go out with joy, and be led forth with peace: the mountains and the hills shall break forth before you into singing, and all the trees of the field shall clap their hands.*

One of the main ways God leads Christians is to lead them by the peace they have by the Spirit of God that is in them, if they have a joyful attitude about following God and His ways as best they know how. It is God's desire to lead His people. Jesus said (John 10:27):

John 10: 27 *My sheep hear my voice, and I know them, and they follow me:*

God is capable of teaching us:

John 14:26 *But the Comforter, which is the Holy Ghost, whom the Father will send in my name, he shall teach you all things, and bring all things to your remembrance, whatsoever I have said unto you.*

The **SECOND TRUMPET** announcement is recorded in Rev 8.8-9:

Rev 8:8 *And the second angel sounded, and as it were a great mountain burning with fire was cast into the sea: and the third part of the sea became blood;.*

Rev 8:9 *And the third part of the creatures which were in the sea, and had life, died; and the third part of the ships were destroyed.*

The associated notes from my previous book "Understanding the Book of Revelation" are:

Notes from 8:8 "The SECOND TRUMPET is sounded. Another judgment is announced upon the Earth. The two witness have power to turn the waters into blood- Rev 11:6 notes. A third part of the seas is turned into blood."

Notes from 8:9 "A third part of the creatures of the sea die, and a third part of the ships are destroyed."

An example of a prophet proclaiming this judgment and turning waters, streams, rivers, ponds throughout an entire country into blood is the example of Moses in Exodus 7:19-20 above.

In the course of proclaiming God's judgments and God's words, Prophets and Apostles shall come from around the world, and eventually converge on Jerusalem, where they will later be killed. At the beginning of the Church Age, Christianity was spread to the world by the Apostles and Prophets, beginning in Jerusalem. They went forth walking in the power of God, with God working miracles through them to prove their words and to glorify His name. At the end of the Church Age, Apostles and Prophets will bring Christianity back to Jerusalem, walking in the same power of God, with God working miracles through them to prove their words and to glorify His name. According to Acts 1:8-9, among the last things Jesus spoke unto his disciples, who would later become Apostles and Prophets, was:

Acts 1:8 *But ye shall receive power, after that the Holy Ghost is come upon you: and ye shall be witnesses unto me both in Jerusalem, and in all Judaea, and in Samaria, and unto the uttermost part of the earth.*

Acts 1:9 *And when he had spoken these things, while they beheld, he was taken up; and a cloud received him out of their sight.*

In the end times, the blessing will be returned to Jerusalem. Present day Apostles and Prophets shall come from the uttermost part of the Earth, returning to Israel and to Jerusalem.

In addition to announcing God's judgments upon the Earth, these two witnesses shall have power from God to convince mankind of their sins, of impending punishment, and of the supremacy of God and His only begotten son - Jesus Christ.

Rev 11:6 *These have power to shut heaven, that it rain not in the days of their prophecy: and have power over waters to turn them to blood, and to smite the earth with all plagues, as often as they will.*

The time of their testimony, with the full power and anointing of their ministry, will begin after they are sealed by the angels of God (as explained above) approximately seven years before the Second Coming of Jesus Christ. During the time of their testimony (about 3 ½ years or 1260 days) they shall have supernatural-spiritual-power to defend themselves against all comers:

Rev 11:5 *And if any man will hurt them, fire proceedeth out of their mouth, and devoureth their enemies: and if any man will hurt them, he must in this manner be killed.*

Note, in Rev 11:5 above, the term "if any man" is translated from the Greek, Strong's number 1536, and actually means "whoever or whatever", not just any human being. These two witnesses have the power to resist all enemies: human, supernatural, spiritual, demonic or "whatever". Eventually, the world will recognize them, even though unwillingly, because later when the time of their testimony has been completed and they are eventually killed by satanic forces, the world will rejoice over their deaths (the world must have known them to be rejoicing over their death):

> Rev 11:10 *And they that dwell upon the earth shall rejoice over them, and make merry, and shall send gifts one to another; because these two prophets tormented them that dwelt on the earth.*

As well as pronouncing God's judgments upon the Earth, the two witnesses shall attempt to expose Mystery, Babylon the Great, the Roman Catholic Church and its Pope who will become the False Prophet. These two witnesses will have signs, miracles, and wonders accompanying their ministry, God co-laboring with them, just like in Mark 16:

> Mark 16:19 *So then after the Lord had spoken unto them, he was received up into heaven, and sat on the right hand of God.*
> Mark 16:20 *And they went forth, and preached every where, the Lord working with them, and confirming the word with signs following. Amen.*

A little later, there will be a war in Heaven in which Satan and his fallen angels will be permanently cast out (Rev 12:7-10). This is the **THIRD TRUMPET**, described in Rev 8:10-11.

> Rev 8:10 *And the third angel sounded, and there fell a great star from heaven, burning as it were a lamp, and it fell upon the third part of the rivers, and upon the fountains of waters;*
> Rev 8:11 *And the name of the star is called Wormwood: and the third part of the waters became wormwood; and many men died of the waters, because they were made bitter.*

This is a future event, but before the Second Coming of Jesus to the Earth. (Endnote 7) Michael leads the angels of God against Satan and his angels. Satan and his angels will be defeated, and there will no longer be a place for them in Heaven. Satan (the devil and the deceiver of mankind) and his angels are then cast out of heaven completely and permanently.

They are cast down to the realm of the Earth A proclamation is made in Heaven. It means God's power is now uncontested in heaven, the enemy has been cast out. Also note, that the angel or being making the proclamation considers the accused (the people of the Church on Earth) to be brethren of himself and the other angels of God (Rev 12:10).

> Rev 12:7 *And there was war in heaven: Michael and his angels fought against the dragon; and the dragon fought and his angels,*
> Rev 12:8 *And prevailed not; neither was their place found any more in heaven.*
> Rev 12:9 *And the great dragon was cast out, that old serpent, called the Devil, and Satan, which deceiveth the whole world: he was cast out into the earth, and his angels were cast out with him.*
> Rev 12:10 *And I heard a loud voice saying in heaven, Now is come salvation, and strength, and the kingdom of our God, and the power of his Christ: for the accuser of our brethren is cast down, which accused them before our God day and night.*
> Rev 12:11 *And they overcame him by the blood of the Lamb, and by the word of their testimony; and they loved not their lives unto the death.*
> Rev 12:12 *Therefore rejoice, ye heavens, and ye that dwell in them. Woe to the inhabiters of the earth and of the sea! for the devil is come down unto you, having great wrath, because he knoweth that he hath but a short time.*
> Rev 12:13 *And when the dragon saw that he was cast unto the earth, he persecuted the woman which brought forth the man child.*

Approximately two thousand years ago, Jesus was the sacrificial Lamb of God, shedding His blood for us, being sacrificed for our sins. The followers of Jesus will overcome Satan and his angels after they come down upon the earth because of Rev 12:11 (above):

a. the blood of the Lamb/Jesus (forgiveness/cleansing of sin)

1 John 1:7 *But if we walk in the light, as he is in the light, we have fellowship one with another, and the blood of Jesus Christ his Son cleanseth us from all sin.*

b. the word of their testimony (their confession of faith in Jesus),

Romans 10:9 *That if thou shalt confess with thy mouth the Lord Jesus, and shalt believe in thine heart that God hath raised him from the dead, thou shalt be saved.*
Romans 10:10 *For with the heart man believeth unto righteousness; and with the mouth confession is made unto salvation.*

c. they loved not their own lives (they were led by the Spirit of God, not by their own fleshly desires) even unto their deaths. This has been the history of the Church before also, with persecution and martyrdom happening throughout the Church age.

According to Rev 12:12 (above) another proclamation is made in heaven. Heaven is told to rejoice. But, the inhabitants of the Earth are told that there will be woe because Satan will come down among us.

Rev 12:13 *And when the dragon saw that he was cast unto the earth, he persecuted the woman which brought forth the man child.*

Satan tries to persecute or capture the woman of Rev 12:13. This woman is the true Christian Church: those that are truly born again Christians. They are washed by the blood of and forgiven by Jesus Christ. This Church is not a denomination or a religion, but is comprised of those people who have a personal relationship with Jesus, believe in and trust in Him for their salvation.

John 14:6 *Jesus saith unto him, I am the way, the truth, and the life: no man cometh unto the Father, but by me.*

Rom 10: 9 *That if thou shalt confess with thy mouth the Lord Jesus, and shalt believe in thine heart that God hath raised him from the dead, thou shalt be saved.*
Rom 10:10 *For with the heart man believeth unto righteousness; and with the mouth confession is made unto salvation.*

Although Satan and his fallen angels will come down among us, God will not let him be unchallenged. The two witnesses-the Apostles and Prophets of God-will have already been sealed by God and cannot be overcome by any Satanic forces during the remaining time of their testimony, as stated above. At that time, the powers of Heaven and Hell will meet, here upon the Earth, in the presence of mankind, and there will be intense spiritual warfare. The powers of Heaven shall be displayed by the two witnesses, and the powers of Hell will be displayed by the followers of Satan. Pertaining to the two witnesses, it is written:

Rev 11:4 *These are the two olive trees, and the two candlesticks standing before the God of the earth.*
Rev 11:5 *And if any man will hurt them, fire proceedeth out of their mouth, and devoureth their enemies: and if any man will hurt them, he must in this manner be killed.*

As explained fully in my previous book "Understanding the Book of Revelation", the two olive trees represent the two witnesses and they stand BEFORE AND IN DIRECT OPPOSITION TO the god of this Earth (Satan).

Notes from 11:4 "These two witnesses are called candlesticks (or lampstands) because they hold the light (Holy Spirit) of God (in themselves) up for all the world to see. They are light in the darkness of the world. They are also the two olive trees. The first is the natural olive tree meaning God's chosen people of the Old Testament: the Jews. The second olive tree is the grafted in olive tree, meaning the Gentiles. (Romans ch. 11:24) These two witnesses are called the two olive trees because these individuals may be of either Jewish or non-Jewish descent (see chapter 7:4 notes).

> Romans 11:24 *For if thou wert cut out of the olive tree which is wild by nature, and wert grafted contrary to nature into a good olive tree: how much more shall these, which be the natural {branches}, be grafted into their own olive tree?*

They stand before-<u>against and in direct opposition to- the god of this Earth (world)-Satan.</u>

The word used for God in the Greek here is "THEOS" (Strong's Concordance # 2316). This term is used throughout the New Testament, including 2 Cor 4:4 (quoted below and clearly meaning Satan in this usage) and here in Rev 11:4 also. Strong's Concordance defines this word as meaning: a deity, the supreme divinity, a magistrate, god, godly, <u>or</u> godward.

> 2 Corinthians 4:4 *In whom the god of this world hath blinded the minds of them which believe not, lest the light of the glorious gospel of Christ, who is the image of God, should shine unto them.*"

Notes from 11:5 "These two witnesses shall defend themselves by speaking the power of God, in the name of Jesus Christ, from their mouths, causing destruction upon their enemies. They shall not need or use physical weapons to defend themselves. This "Army of God" shall go forth invincible (during the time of their testimony-verse 7), with more power in their words than all the armies of this world have in all their weapons. The power of God (through them), and the powers of Hell shall meet here on this Earth, in the presence of mankind. This will happen before Jesus' Second Coming."

The powers of witches and warlocks and the occult will also increase, but they shall not be able to overcome the powers of God, just as in the days of Moses before Pharoah:

> Exodus 7:10 *And Moses and Aaron went in unto Pharaoh, and they did so as the LORD had commanded: and Aaron cast down his rod before Pharaoh, and before his servants, and it became a serpent.*
> Exodus 7:11 *Then Pharaoh also called the wise men and the sorcerers: now the magicians of Egypt, they also did in like manner with their enchantments.*
> Exodus 7:12 *For they cast down every man his rod, and they became serpents: but Aaron's rod swallowed up their rods.*

However, the people in the middle will soon be unprotected, and will have to begin to make choices, favoring or choosing one side or the other. If they choose to follow Satan and his followers they will initially be un-harassed, having chosen physical peace and comfort. Many will do this, including approximately 1/3 of the Christians. The **FOURTH TRUMPET** is written in Rev 8:12. However, those that do choose Satan will eventually suffer God's wrath and damnation.

> Rev 8:12 *And the fourth angel sounded, and the third part of the sun was smitten, and the third part of the moon, and the third part of the stars; so as the third part of them was darkened, and the day shone not for a third part of it, and the night likewise.*

This is explained in my earlier book "Understanding the Book of Revelation" in the notes for Rev 8:12, the fourth trumpet, as follows:

"The <u>FOURTH TRUMPET</u> is sounded. A third part of the sun, moon, and stars are darkened. And the day and night were not distinguishable for the third part of them. This fourth trumpet is very sad in its' meaning. Revelation chapter 12 explained the Woman (Church) being clothed with the sun, and standing on the moon with 12 stars around her head. This fourth trumpet is saying that a third of the Church will be darkened (spiritually) and will no longer shine the light of Christ. This 1/3 of the Church is, or becomes, lukewarm, and undistinguishable from the rest of the world. Jesus said, as recorded by John in Revelation 3:14-16.

> Rev 3:14 *And unto the angel of the church of the Laodiceans write; These things saith the Amen, the faithful and true witness, the beginning of the creation of God;*
> Rev 3:15 *I know thy works, that thou art neither cold nor hot: I would thou wert cold or hot.*
> Rev 3:16 *So then because thou art lukewarm, and neither cold nor hot, I will spue thee out of my mouth.*

These people reject the moving of the Holy Spirit and His gifts through God's servants. They choose to remain comfortable and acceptable to the world. They do not choose to take a stand for Jesus in the face of persecution, embarrassment, or worse. They will not walk in faith, or be conformed to the image of Jesus, and they will not accept the testimony of God's two groups of witnesses that He sends-the Apostles and Prophets (explained in ch 11 notes)."

God never desired or intended mankind to be lukewarm towards Him, but He wants them to make the choice to be for or against Him, or if they refuse to choose or if they choose to be lukewarm, He will reject them. The time is soon coming when all mankind will have to choose. Other Bible verses also show this same nature of God.

1Ki 18:21 *And Elijah came unto all the people, and said, How long halt ye between two opinions? if the LORD be God, follow him: but if Baal, then follow him. And the people answered him not a word.*

Mat 10:36 *And a man's foes shall be they of his own household.*
Mat 10:37 *He that loveth father or mother more than me is not worthy of me: and he that loveth son or daughter more than me is not worthy of me.*
Mat 10:38 *And he that taketh not his cross, and followeth after me, is not worthy of me.*
Mat 10:39 *He that findeth his life shall lose it: and he that loseth his life for my sake shall find it.*

CHAPTER FOUR

The Rise of the Antichrist-
The Fifth Trumpet

As just shown in the previous chapter, Revelation 8:12 calls this falling away of Christians the sounding of the fourth angel, or the fourth trumpet.

Paul said that the Antichrist, the "man of sin", shall arise after a falling away.

> 2 Th:2:2 *That ye be not soon shaken in mind, or be troubled, neither by spirit, nor by word, nor by letter as from us, as that the day of Christ is at hand.*
>
> 2 Th:2:3 *Let no man deceive you by any means: for that day shall not come, except there come a falling away first, and that man of sin be revealed, the son of perdition;*
>
> 2 Th:2:4 *Who opposeth and exalteth himself above all that is called God, or that is worshipped; so that he as God sitteth in the temple of God, shewing himself that he is God.*

Revelation chapter 9 tells of the sounding of the fifth angel, or the **FIFTH TRUMPET**, and this begins the story of the rise of the Antichrist. He comes from and is the king of the bottomless pit. This bottomless pit is also under the sea, as will be shown. An angel is sent to open the bottomless pit to release this king and his forces from the bottomless pit upon the Earth (verse 1).

> Rev 9:*1 And the fifth angel sounded, and I saw a star fall from heaven unto the earth: and to him was given the key of the bottomless pit.*
> Rev 9:2 *And he opened the bottomless pit; and there arose a smoke out of the pit, as the smoke of a great furnace; and the sun and the air were darkened by reason of the smoke of the pit.*

In Hebrew, the name of this king of the bottomless pit is called Abaddon (destruction) but in Greek he is called Apollyon (meaning destroyer) (Amplified Bible, Rev 9:11).

> Rev 9:11 (Amplified Version) *Over them as king they have the angel of the abyss-of the bottomless pit. In Hebrew his name is Abaddon [destruction], but in Greek he is called Apollyon [destroyer].*

The story of the rise of the beast or Antichrist among mankind is also told in Rev chapter 13, verses 1 through 10. In verse one, the Antichrist is seen arising out of the sea.

> Rev 13:1 ¶ *And I stood upon the sand of the sea, and saw a beast rise up out of the sea, having seven heads and ten horns, and upon his horns ten crowns, and upon his heads the name of blasphemy.*

With the opening of the shaft to the bottomless pit, smoke is released (Rev 9:2 above) and darkens the sun and the atmosphere and hence the moon and the stars also. This is the beginning of the manifestation of the great deception or delusion that is coming upon the Earth.

This king or Antichrist with his forces from the bottomless pit will come up upon the Earth among mankind. The Antichrist is not a man alive and walking the Earth now (in early 2006), for he will come up from the bottomless pit with great notice/signs, with the smoke and the darkening of the sun and atmosphere.

The creatures or beings with the Antichrist have faces that resemble mankind (Rev 9:7) and are "condemned beings", having been condemned and imprisoned by God.

> Rev 9:7 *And the shapes of the locusts were like unto horses prepared unto battle; and on their heads were as it were crowns like gold, and their faces were as the faces of men.*

Although the Antichrist is called an angel in Rev 9:11 above, he is not fully an angel, but a half-breed, being fathered by an angel and born of human women. The book of Jude in verse 6 says that the angels which left their own habitations are bound until judgment day. Therefore, those fallen angels cannot be coming back to Earth before judgment day.

> Jude 6 *And the angels which kept not their first estate, but left their own habitation, he hath reserved in everlasting chains under darkness unto the judgment of the great day.*

The Book of Genesis, chapter 6 tells the story of those angels who left their place in heaven and came to Earth to father children by human women. Half humans, fathered by fallen angels, have existed before and were among the reasons that God flooded the Earth:

> Gen 6:4 ¶ *There were giants in the earth in those days; and also after that, when the sons of God came in unto the daughters of men, and they bare children to them, the same became mighty men which were of old, men of renown.*
> Gen 6:5 *And GOD saw that the wickedness of man was great in the earth, and that every imagination of the thoughts of his heart was only evil continually.*

Gen 6:6 ¶ And it repented the LORD that he had made man on the earth, and it grieved him at his heart.
Gen 6:7 And the LORD said, I will destroy man whom I have created from the face of the earth; both man, and beast, and the creeping thing, and the fowls of the air; for it repenteth me that I have made them.
Gen 6:8 ¶ But Noah found grace in the eyes of the LORD.

The term "sons of God" (verse 4 above) in the Old Testament usage here refers to angels, as is also does in Job chapters 1 and 2.

Job 1:6 Now there was a day when the sons of God came to present themselves before the LORD, and Satan came also among them.

Job 2:1 Again there was a day when the sons of God came to present themselves before the LORD, and Satan came also among them to present himself before the LORD.

Therefore, there have been children of fallen angels who walked the face of the Earth. At this time, with the Antichrist, they are released from the bottomless pit to come up upon the Earth again.

Rev 9:7 And the shapes of the locusts were like unto horses prepared unto battle; and on their heads were as it were crowns like gold, and their faces were as the faces of men.

These half-breed (angel/human) beings definitely had physical bodies. Also, they will have physical bodies when they come back among mankind, or else how could they interact with mankind physically, causing pain and torment as shown in Rev chapter 9 below. These beings also seem to need to have some special flying machines to transport themselves quickly up through the water and through the smoke from the bottomless pit and through the air. These half-breed beings may have been working on advanced technology for thousands of years, and may be the explanation for unidentified flying objects (UFOs) and unidentified submerged objects (USOs).

In the meantime, the two witnesses will continue to speak God's words and judgments upon the Earth, intending to expose the works of darkness, including: 1) exposing the Antichrist; and 2) exposing the Roman Catholic Church as Mystery, Babylon; and 3) to warn of God's impending judgments; seeking to turn all people to Jesus Christ and God.

After the Antichrist's coming, his forces war against the inhabitants of the Earth, to take control of the Earth. This war, or at least this phase of the war, lasts for 5 months. Rev 9:3-11.

Rev 9:3 *And there came out of the smoke locusts upon the earth: and unto them was given power, as the scorpions of the earth have power.*

Rev 9:4 *And it was commanded them that they should not hurt the grass of the earth, neither any green thing, neither any tree; but only those men which have not the seal of God in their foreheads.*

Rev 9:5 *And to them it was given that they should not kill them, but that they should be tormented five months: and their torment was as the torment of a scorpion, when he striketh a man.*

Rev 9:6 *And in those days shall men seek death, and shall not find it; and shall desire to die, and death shall flee from them.*

Rev 9:7 *And the shapes of the locusts were like unto horses prepared unto battle; and on their heads were as it were crowns like gold, and their faces were as the faces of men.*

Rev 9:8 *And they had hair as the hair of women, and their teeth were as the teeth of lions.*

Rev 9:9 *And they had breastplates, as it were breastplates of iron; and the sound of their wings was as the sound of chariots of many horses running to battle.*

Rev 9:10 *And they had tails like unto scorpions, and there were stings in their tails: and their power was to hurt men five months.*

Rev 9:11 *And they had a king over them, which is the angel of the bottomless pit, whose name in the Hebrew tongue is Abaddon, but in the Greek tongue hath his name Apollyon.*

For five months these things torment mankind who do not have the seal of God in their foreheads. (Those that have the seal of God in their foreheads are the two witnesses, Rev 9:4 above, which are still alive at this time. Also, remember Rev 7:3).

> Rev 7:3 *Saying, Hurt not the earth, neither the sea, nor the trees, till we have sealed the servants of our God in their foreheads.*

This five month long war causes the Antichrist and his forces to subdue much of the Earth, and he will eventually take control of the Earth. There shall be a ten nation ruling confederacy formed, three of which will be forced into submission.

> Rev 17:11 *And the beast that was, and is not, even he is the eighth, and is of the seven, and goeth into perdition.*
> Rev 17:12 *And the ten horns which thou sawest are ten kings, which have received no kingdom as yet; but receive power as kings one hour with the beast.*
> Rev 17:13 *These have one mind, and shall give their power and strength unto the beast.*

> Dan 7:24 *And the ten horns out of this kingdom are ten kings that shall arise: and another shall rise after them; and he shall be diverse from the first, and he shall subdue three kings.*
> Dan 7:25 *And he shall speak great words against the most High, and shall wear out the saints of the most High, and think to change times and laws: and they shall be given into his hand until a time and times and the dividing of time.*

The only area that can resist the powers of the Antichrist is that area occupied by the two witnesses, the Apostles and Prophets. This makes the Antichrist hate Jerusalem and Israel even more.

Zech 12:1 ¶ The burden of the word of the LORD for Israel, saith the LORD, which stretcheth forth the heavens, and layeth the foundation of the earth, and formeth the spirit of man within him.

Zech 12:2 Behold, I will make Jerusalem a cup of trembling unto all the people round about, when they shall be in the siege both against Judah and against Jerusalem.

Zech 12:3 And in that day will I make Jerusalem a burdensome stone for all people: all that burden themselves with it shall be cut in pieces, though all the people of the earth be gathered together against it.

Zech 12:4 In that day, saith the LORD, I will smite every horse with astonishment, and his rider with madness: and I will open mine eyes upon the house of Judah, and will smite every horse of the people with blindness.

Zech 12:5 And the governors of Judah shall say in their heart, The inhabitants of Jerusalem shall be my strength in the LORD of hosts their God.

Zech 12:6 In that day will I make the governors of Judah like an hearth of fire among the wood, and like a torch of fire in a sheaf; and they shall devour all the people round about, on the right hand and on the left: and Jerusalem shall be inhabited again in her own place, even in Jerusalem.

Verse 3 says all the people of the earth shall be gathered together against it (Jerusalem). Verse 5 says the governors of Judah shall say in their heart, the inhabitants of Jerusalem (the Apostles and Prophets-the two witnesses) shall be their strength in the LORD of hosts THEIR God (as if the governors of Judah still will not acknowledge yet that the God of the two witnesses-Jesus Christ-is the God of Israel). It will be perfectly clear and demonstrated during those 5 months of war, that the inhabitants of Jerusalem-the two witnesses-will have more power than the Antichrist and will protect their "turf": themselves, those that follow them, and where they live! Though the whole world be under the power of the Antichrist at that time, yet Jerusalem (and perhaps the surrounding areas) will not be. This will be a great sign and wonder to the Jews, that there is power in Jesus Christ, to begin to strongly convince them of His Deity, that Jesus is the Son of God!

> Zech 12:10 *And I will pour upon the house of David, and upon the inhabitants of Jerusalem, the spirit of grace and of supplications: and they shall look upon me whom they have pierced, and they shall mourn for him, as one mourneth for his only son, and shall be in bitterness for him, as one that is in bitterness for his firstborn.*
> Zech 12:11 *In that day shall there be a great mourning in Jerusalem, as the mourning of Hadadrimmon in the valley of Megiddon.*
> Zech 12:12 *And the land shall mourn, every family apart; the family of the house of David apart, and their wives apart; the family of the house of Nathan apart, and their wives apart;*
> Zech 12:13 *The family of the house of Levi apart, and their wives apart; the family of Shimei apart, and their wives apart;*
> Zech 12:14 *All the families that remain, every family apart, and their wives apart.*
> Zech 13:1 ¶ *In that day there shall be a fountain opened to the house of David and to the inhabitants of Jerusalem for sin and for uncleanness.*

Although the Jewish people pierced Jesus (verse 10) when He walked the Earth, they will eventually come to recognize Him as the Messiah, and they will mourn for Him. They will mourn for having rejected Him for so many years. They will mourn apart (repentance and salvation are a personal-individual-experience). Many Jewish people will repent and accept Jesus Christ as their savior-as the Messiah.

CHAPTER FIVE

The Sixth Trumpet
and
The Great Deception

After approximately the first 5 months of the Antichrist on the Earth are completed, God allows the release of four angels (Rev 9:14) which signifies the beginning of the time that the Antichrist is allowed to kill people. This is the announcement of the **SIXTH TRUMPET**.

> Rev 9:14 *Saying to the sixth angel which had the trumpet, Loose the four angels which are bound in the great river Euphrates.*
>
> Rev 9:15 *And the four angels were loosed, which were prepared for an hour, and a day, and a month, and a year, for to slay the third part of men.*
>
> Rev 9:16 *And the number of the army of the horsemen were two hundred thousand thousand: and I heard the number of them.*
>
> Rev 9:17 *And thus I saw the horses in the vision, and them that sat on them, having breastplates of fire, and of jacinth, and brimstone: and the heads of the horses were as the heads of lions; and out of their mouths issued fire and smoke and brimstone.*
>
> Rev 9:18 *By these three was the third part of men killed, by the fire, and by the smoke, and by the brimstone, which issued out of their mouths.*

Rev 9:19 *For their power is in their mouth, and in their tails: for their tails were like unto serpents, and had heads, and with them they do hurt.*

Rev 9:20 *And **the rest of the men** which were not killed by these plagues yet **repented not**................*

The Antichrist is now allowed to kill people. At the beginning of this period, the Antichrist first kills his enemies-the two witnesses-not his friends. The time allotted for the testimony of the two witnesses will now be over. They will have testified for three and one half years, including the 5 month long war, during which the Antichrist will have been upon the Earth, up to this point.

Rev 11:7 <u>*And when they shall have finished their testimony, the beast that ascendeth out of the bottomless pit shall make war against them, and shall overcome them, and kill them.*</u>

Rev 11:8 *And their dead bodies shall lie in the street of the great city, which spiritually is called Sodom and Egypt, where also our Lord was crucified.*

Rev 11:9 *And they of the people and kindreds and tongues and nations shall see their dead bodies three days and an half, and shall not suffer their dead bodies to be put in graves.*

Rev 11:10 *And they that dwell upon the earth shall rejoice over them, and make merry, and shall send gifts one to another; because these two prophets tormented them that dwelt on the earth.*

Carefully consider Rev 11:7 above: **it is the beast that ascendeth out of the bottomless pit that makes war against and kills the two witnesses**. This is Abaddon/Apollyon/Antichrist (Rev 9:1&11).

Rev 9:*1And the fifth angel sounded, and I saw a star fall from heaven unto the earth: and to him was given the key of the bottomless pit.*

Rev 9:11 (Amplified Version) *Over them as king they have the angel of the abyss-of the bottomless pit. In Hebrew his name is Abaddon [destruction], but in Greek he is called Apollyon [destroyer].*

At this time, the Antichrist does not kill his followers, or even kill the undecided, because he is after something much more important: their eternal souls, not just their physical lives. He wants to deceive them into following him, swearing allegiance to him, or doing homage or worshipping him.

This begins the unlimited power of the Antichrist upon the Earth, lasting for another three and one half years (Rev 13:4-8).

Rev 13:4 *And they worshipped the dragon which gave power unto the beast: and they worshipped the beast, saying, Who is like unto the beast? Who is able to make war with him?*

Rev 13:5 *And there was given unto him a mouth speaking great things and blasphemies; and power was given unto him to continue forty and two months.*

Rev 13:6 *And he opened his mouth in blasphemy against God, to blaspheme his name, and his tabernacle, and them that dwell in heaven.*

Rev 13:7 *And it was given unto him to make war with the saints, and to overcome them: and power was given him over all kindreds, and tongues, and nations.*

Rev 13:8 *And all that dwell upon the earth shall worship him, whose names are not written in the book of life of the Lamb slain from the foundation of the world.*

God is going to allow a great deception to come upon the Earth. In 2 Thessalonians chapter 2 verses 1-3 and verse 11, the Bible tells of a great deception or lie which God will send or allow to come upon the Earth.

This great deception will come upon the Earth before Jesus' Second Coming and before Jesus gathers us to Him.

> 2 Th 2:1 ¶ *Now we beseech you, brethren, by the coming of our Lord Jesus Christ, and by our gathering together unto him,*
> 2 Th 2:2 *That ye be not soon shaken in mind, or be troubled, neither by spirit, nor by word, nor by letter as from us, as that the day of Christ is at hand.*
> 2 Th 2:3 ¶ *Let no man deceive you by any means: for that day shall not come, except there come a falling away first, and that man of sin be revealed, the son of perdition;*
> 2 Th 2:4 *Who opposeth and exalteth himself above all that is called God, or that is worshipped; so that he as God sitteth in the temple of God, shewing himself that he is God.*
> 2 Th 2:5 *Remember ye not, that, when I was yet with you, I told you these things?*
> 2 Th 2:6 *And now ye know what withholdeth that he might be revealed in his time.*
> 2 Th 2:7 *For the mystery of iniquity doth already work: only he who now letteth will let, until he be taken out of the way.*
> 2 Th 2:8 *And then shall that Wicked be revealed, whom the Lord shall consume with the spirit of his mouth, and shall destroy with the brightness of his coming:*
> 2 Th 2:9 *Even him, whose coming is after the working of Satan with all power and signs and lying wonders,*
> 2 Th 2:10 *And with all deceivableness of unrighteousness in them that perish; because they received not the love of the truth, that they might be saved.*
> 2 Th 2:11 *And for this cause God shall send them strong delusion, that they should believe a lie:*
> 2 Th 2:12 *That they all might be damned who believed not the truth, but had pleasure in unrighteousness.*

The Great Deception that the Antichrist will attempt to put into place is this: the **ANTICHRIST WILL CLAIM TO BE JESUS CHRIST-THE MESSIAH.** He will compare his coming with the prophesied Second Coming of Christ, as described in Matt 24 and Mark 13:

> Mat 24:27 *For as the lightning cometh out of the east, and shineth even unto the west; so shall also the coming of the Son of man be.*
> Mat 24:28 *For wheresoever the carcase is, there will the eagles be gathered together.*
> Mat 24:29 *Immediately after the tribulation of those days shall the sun be darkened, and the moon shall not give her light, and the stars shall fall from heaven, and the powers of the heavens shall be shaken:*
> Mat 24:30 *And then shall appear the sign of the Son of man in heaven: and then shall all the tribes of the earth mourn, and they shall see the Son of man coming in the clouds of heaven with power and great glory.*
> Mat 24:31 *And he shall send his angels with a great sound of a trumpet, and they shall gather together his elect from the four winds, from one end of heaven to the other.*
>
> Mark 13:24 ¶ *But in those days, after that tribulation, the sun shall be darkened, and the moon shall not give her light,*
> Mark 13:25 *And the stars of heaven shall fall, and the powers that are in heaven shall be shaken.*
> Mark 13:26 *And then shall they see the Son of man coming in the clouds with great power and glory.*

Remember, immediately before the Antichrist and his forces appear, the smoke from the bottomless pit will darken the sun and the atmosphere and the moon and stars. The lie the Antichrist will want us to believe is that his coming this fulfills the prophecy of Mat 24:29, Second Coming of Christ, the coming of the Jewish Messiah. This Antichrist (or Christ Impersonator, Imitation Christ, or False Christ) will want us to believe that he is Jesus Christ, and that those who do not believe in him are the carcasses (spiritually dead people) of Mat 24:28, and that the eagles of the same verse are his forces as they gather to do battle against those who will not receive him as the returning Christ. He will want us to believe that Mat 24:27 means that the whole Earth will see the Second Coming and that this is fulfilled by the whole Earth seeing his coming. The Antichrist will want us to believe that Mat 24:30 is fulfilled by his coming in the clouds with great power. Eventually, he will want us to believe that Mat 24:31 will be fulfilled by sending his forces to get people to swear allegiance to or worship him.

As is beginning to be seen, this Antichrist is more that just anti-Christ, he is also an Imitation Christ, a deceiver, a half-human, and part of a great deception allowed to come upon the Earth. The Apostle Paul said in 2 Thessalonians chapter 2, that the real Jesus Christ would not come and we would not be gathered together unto Jesus (verse 3) until after a falling away and that man of sin (the Antichrist) be revealed. Verse 4 continues to say that this man of sin (Antichrist) will (later) sit in the temple of God, claiming that he is God (actually claiming to be Christ). As stated earlier, this will all happen before the real Second Coming of Jesus Christ and our gathering unto Him.

> 2 Th 2:3 ¶ *Let no man deceive you by any means: for that day shall not come, except there come a falling away first, and that man of sin be revealed, the son of perdition;*
> 2 Th 2:4 *Who opposeth and exalteth himself above all that is called God, or that is worshipped; so that he as God sitteth in the temple of God, shewing himself that he is God.*

This very believable deception is coming upon the Earth, before the real Second Coming of the real Jesus Christ:

> Mark 13:22 *For false Christs and false prophets shall rise, and shall shew signs and wonders, to seduce, if it were possible, even the elect.*
> Mark 13:23 *But take ye heed: behold, I have foretold you all things.*

Mark 13:24 *But in those days, after that tribulation, the sun shall be darkened, and the moon shall not give her light,*
Mark 13:25 *And the stars of heaven shall fall, and the powers that are in heaven shall be shaken.*
Mark 13:26 *And then shall they see the Son of man coming in the clouds with great power and glory.*

2 Thes 2:11 *And for this cause God shall send them strong delusion, that they should believe a lie:*
2 Thes 2:12 *That they all might be damned who believed not the truth, but had pleasure in unrighteousness.*

This Imitation Christ-the Antichrist-will eventually convince the Pope and the leadership of the Roman Catholic Church that he is the Christ and that they have done a good job of holding his temporal crown for him. The "woman" of Rev chapter 17 as explained earlier is clearly the city/center representing the Roman Catholic Church. The Antichrist will then take over the Roman Catholic Church, with the approval, blessing and backing of the Pope, Pope Benedict 16th, who will then become the False Prophet in declaring the Antichrist to be the actual Christ.

This Antichrist thus will become the apparent visible "divine (in claim only)" leader of the Roman Catholic Church, becoming the 8th king to control this religious kingdom's headquarters-the country of the Vatican. Therefore, the Antichrist becomes kind of like an 8th Pope, except that the 7th Pope (Pope Benedict 16th) is still alive. As explained in the notes of my previous book, "Understanding the Book of Revelation": for Rev 17:11

Notes for for Rev 17:11: "This is the beast (spirit) that was, is not, and shall be, and shall go into perdition-Abaddon/Apollyon-the Antichrist (see Rev 17:8 notes). He is the eighth, to control this religious kingdom's headquarters-the Vatican. He is of the seven, because he controlled them through his spirit before he came physically. However, his fate is sealed, and he will eventually be cast into Hell. Note that the False Prophet is on the scene physically and is in position (the office of the Pope/King of Vatican) before the Antichrist (the 8th) physically comes and rules over him."

Note that the Roman Catholic faith believes that the Pope is the "Vicar of Christ" or the spokesman for Christ on the Earth, reigning over the Christian world for Christ. But the Bible says that Christ is the head of the Church, (Eph 5:23-"even as Christ is the head of the church") so it is quite logical that Christ would come to claim what has been held for Him until His return. However, this Antichrist is not the real Christ and the Roman Catholic Church is not the real Christian Church although some Catholics are definitely very good Christians. (The real Christian Church is made up of all Christians, no matter what religion they may subscribe to.)

The actual verse from the Bible about this Antichrist or eighth leader/Pope/King of the Vatican is Rev 17:11.

> Rev 17:11 *And the beast that was, and is not, even he is the eighth, and is of the seven, and goeth into perdition.*

Also, the people of Earth shall wonder when they see the one who "ascends out of the bottomless pit". The Amplified Bible-Rev 17:8 says they "will be astonished when they look at the beast". From the King James Version of the Bible:

> Rev 17:7 *And the angel said unto me, Wherefore didst thou marvel? I will tell thee the mystery of the woman, and of the beast that carrieth her, which hath the seven heads and ten horns.*
> Rev 17:8 *The beast that thou sawest was, and is not; and shall ascend out of the bottomless pit, and go into perdition: and they that dwell on the earth shall <u>wonder</u>, whose names were not written in the book of life from the foundation of the world, <u>when they behold</u> the beast that was, and is not, and yet is.*

Part of this deception may be that the Antichrist might look like the man on the cloth of the Shroud of Turin, maintained for so long by the Roman Catholic Church. "On May 4, 2005, Bishop Severino Poletto, Archbishop of Turin, unveiled the newly remodeled reliquiary in Turin's Cathedral of St. John the Baptist, where the Shroud is permanently stored." (from Internet; http://www.shroud.com/latebrak.htm, Oct 27, 2005). This cloth could be kind of like a "fingerprint" of the physical body of the Antichrist. People would be astonished when they see the similarity.

Remember, this beast (Rev 17:8 above), the Antichrist, was a man, a half human being, fathered by a fallen angel, who lived upon the Earth , but who then went into perdition (in the Earth) and shall come again, alive and in power, ascending up from the bottomless pit.

> Rev 9:11 *And they had a king over them, which is the angel of the bottomless pit, whose name in the Hebrew tongue is Abaddon, but in the Greek tongue hath his name Apollyon.*

This is the explanation of the term in Rev 17:8 *"that was, and is not, and shall ascend out of the bottomless pit"* and Rev 17:11: *"And the beast that was, and is not, even he is…"*. He cannot be killed. This is also part of the reason of Rev 13:4 where it says "who is like unto the beast?" and "who is able to make war with him". The other reason they say that is because of the powerful forces at his command.

> Rev 13:4 …… *and they worshipped the beast, saying, Who is <u>like</u> unto the beast? who is <u>able</u> to make war with him?*

In the Book of Daniel, it is said that the kingdom of the last days Antichrist is different from all the kingdoms before it. In particular, this can be referring to its last King, the Antichrist.

> Dan 7:7 *After this I saw in the night visions, and behold a fourth beast, dreadful and terrible, and strong exceedingly; and it had*

great iron teeth: it devoured and brake in pieces, and stamped the residue with the feet of it: <u>and it was diverse from all the beasts that were before it</u>; and it had ten horns.

Dan 7:23 *Thus he said, The fourth beast shall be the fourth kingdom upon earth, which shall be <u>diverse from all kingdoms</u>, and shall devour the whole earth, and shall tread it down, and break it in pieces.*
Dan 7:24 *And the ten horns out of this kingdom are ten kings that shall arise: and another shall rise after them; and <u>he shall be diverse from the first</u>, and he shall subdue three kings.*
Dan 7:25 *And he shall speak great words against the most High, and shall wear out the saints of the most High, and think to change times and laws: and they shall be given into his hand until a time and times and the dividing of time.*

In Daniel, chapter 2, it says that this different powerful kingdom (the fourth of Dan 7:23) which shall come will be like feet and toes of iron mixed with clay.

Dan 2:40 *And the fourth kingdom shall be strong as iron: forasmuch as iron breaketh in pieces and subdueth all things: and as iron that breaketh all these, shall it break in pieces and bruise.*
Dan 2:41 *And whereas thou sawest the feet and toes, part of potters' clay, and part of iron, the kingdom shall be divided; but there shall be in it of the strength of the iron, forasmuch as thou sawest the iron mixed with miry clay.*
Dan 2:42 *And as the toes of the feet were part of iron, and part of clay, so the kingdom shall be partly strong, and partly broken.*
Dan 2:43 *And whereas thou sawest iron mixed with miry clay, they shall mingle themselves with the seed of men: but they shall not cleave one to another, even as iron is not mixed with clay.*
Dan 2:44 *And in the days of these kings shall the God of heaven set up a kingdom, which shall never be destroyed: and the kingdom*

shall not be left to other people, but it shall break in pieces and consume all these kingdoms, and it shall stand for ever.

This mixing is also like the mixing of those half-breed beings that come up from the bottomless pit, and those that verse 43 says are the seed of men (the human race). Both "races" may work for the Antichrist, but "they shall not cleave one to another", meaning that they will not have a close continuing personal/emotional relationship. They will choose not to. Also, humans are made of clay/dirt/dust and are compared to "clay" (verse 41 and 43) and this same comparison is made in Job 10:9, 13:12, 33:6 and Is 45:9, 64:8. The iron part of this represents the strong or "seemingly invincible" ones from the bottomless pit.

Of the Roman Catholic Church leadership, with its False Prophet fully assisting the Antichrist, the Bible says "Babylon is fallen, is fallen"

Rev 14:6 ¶ And I saw another angel fly in the midst of heaven, having the everlasting gospel to preach unto them that dwell on the earth, and to every nation, and kindred, and tongue, and people,

Rev 14:7 Saying with a loud voice, Fear God, and give glory to him; for the hour of his judgment is come: and worship him that made heaven, and earth, and the sea, and the fountains of waters.

Rev 14:8 And there followed another angel, saying, <u>Babylon is fallen, is fallen, that great city</u>, because she made all nations drink of the wine of the wrath of her fornication.

Rev 14:9 And the third angel followed them, saying with a loud voice, If any man worship the beast and his image, and receive his mark in his forehead, or in his hand,

Rev 14:10 The same shall drink of the wine of the wrath of God, which is poured out without mixture into the cup of his indignation; and he shall be tormented with fire and brimstone in the presence of the holy angels, and in the presence of the Lamb:

Rev 14:11 *And the smoke of their torment ascendeth up for ever and ever: and they have no rest day nor night, who worship the beast and his image, and whosoever receiveth the mark of his name.*

Rev 14:12 *Here is the patience of the saints: here are they that keep the commandments of God, and the faith of Jesus.,*

Rev 18:1 *And after these things I saw another angel come down from heaven, having great power; and the earth was lightened with his glory.*

Rev 18:2 *And he cried mightily with a strong voice, saying, <u>Babylon the great is fallen, is fallen</u>, and is become the habitation of devils, and the hold of every foul spirit, and a cage of every unclean and hateful bird.*

Rev 18:3 *For all nations have drunk of the wine of the wrath of her fornication, and the kings of the earth have committed fornication with her, and the merchants of the earth are waxed rich through the abundance of her delicacies.*

CHAPTER SIX

Two Witnesses' Resurrection
and
Unmasking the Antichrist

The Antichrist (who is not Satan) is going to be claiming that the two witnesses were deceivers, following Satan and that the scriptures warned people that those kinds of false prophets would appear in the latter days. He will even claim that the people and even parents of those two witness should have thrust them through and killed them when they could, in accordance with scriptures like Zech 13:2-3.

> Zech 13:2 *And it shall come to pass in that day, saith the LORD of hosts, that I will cut off the names of the idols out of the land, and they shall no more be remembered: and also I will cause the prophets and the unclean spirit to pass out of the land.*
> Zech 13:3 *And it shall come to pass, that when any shall yet prophesy, then his father and his mother that begat him shall say unto him, Thou shalt not live; for thou speakest lies in the name of the LORD: and his father and his mother that begat him shall thrust him through when he prophesieth.*

However, these scripture are talking about false prophets, heathen prophets, diviners or fortune tellers, etc. and not God's true prophets.

However, his victory is short lived, because God will prove who is telling the truth:

> Rev 11:9 *And they of the people and kindreds and tongues and nations shall see their dead bodies three days and an half, and shall not suffer their dead bodies to be put in graves.*
> Rev 11:10 *And they that dwell upon the earth shall rejoice over them, and make merry, and shall send gifts one to another; because these two prophets tormented them that dwelt on the earth.*
> Rev 11:11 *And after three days and an half the Spirit of life from God entered into them, and they stood upon their feet; and great fear fell upon them which saw them.*
> Rev 11:12 *And they heard a great voice from heaven saying unto them, Come up hither. And they ascended up to heaven in a cloud; and their enemies beheld them.*
> Rev 11:13 *And the same hour was there a great earthquake, and the tenth part of the city fell, and in the earthquake were slain of men seven thousand: and the remnant were affrighted, and gave glory to the God of heaven.*

From my previous book "Understanding the Book of Revelation", the following was written as explanations for the above verses:

> Notes for Rev 11:10 People of the Earth shall rejoice that these prophets are dead. People of the earth felt tormented by them because God, by announcements and declarations through them, brought conviction, plagues, lack of rain, etc. upon the ungodly people for their sins, calling for them to repent and to turn whole heartedly to God and Jesus.

> Notes for Rev 11:11 After three and a half days, these bodies are resurrected from the dead. God shall cause them to rise from the dead. These shall have done the deeds of Christ in their lifetime, coming unto a maturity of walking in the fullness of the Holy

Spirit within them (as Jesus did), and they shall be raised from the dead (just as Jesus Christ was raised from the dead). And those that shall see them shall fear.

Notes for Rev 11:12 These apostles and prophets are then called up and ascend up into heaven, in plain sight of all. From this point on, people on Earth know beyond any doubt, that what these apostles and prophets said was true and was verified by Almighty God.

Notes for Rev 11:13 And there was a great earthquake accompanying these events, and many believed the words of the apostles and prophets (upon seeing these things) and glorified God.

With this unmasking of his identity, the Antichrist will try harder to convince people to follow him, trying to convince people of his imitation Second Coming-that He is the Christ. He will even become ruthless. His power is also now uncontested, so he can also use force if necessary to convince them and get them to agree, although he would rather be reserved and deceive people to get them to follow him willingly.

With Jerusalem no longer being protected by the power of the two witnesses, the Antichrist will then take Jerusalem to gain control of the Temple area, claiming to take his rightful throne and temple on Earth.

Zech 14:1 ¶ *Behold, the day of the LORD cometh, and thy spoil shall be divided in the midst of thee.*
Zech 14:2 *For I will gather all nations against Jerusalem to battle; and the city shall be taken, and the houses rifled, and the women ravished; and half of the city shall go forth into captivity, and the residue of the people shall not be cut off from the city.*

The Antichrist (and Satan) hates the Jewish people and will allow the Jewish portion of the city to be plundered and the Jewish people to be taken captive and removed from the city. He may say that it is their judgment for having killed and rejected him. He will not restrain the autocracies that will be committed. Many of these Jewish people may have already accepted Jesus as their Messiah by this time, or at least have seen many others do so.

In the Book of Revelation, chapter 11 verse 2 says that the holy city (Jerusalem) will be trodden down of the gentiles for 42 months.

> Rev 11:2 *But the court which is without the temple leave out, and measure it not; for it is given unto the Gentiles: and the holy city shall they tread under foot forty and two months.*

Remember, even Satan wanted to be exalted/worshipped and to be "like" God (Is 14:12-14).

> Is14:12 *How art thou fallen from heaven, O Lucifer, son of the morning! how art thou cut down to the ground, which didst weaken the nations!*
> Is14:13 *For thou hast said in thine heart, I will ascend into heaven, I will exalt my throne above the stars of God: I will sit also upon the mount of the congregation, in the sides of the north:*
> Is14:14 *I will ascend above the heights of the clouds; I will be like the most High.*

The Antichrist will at least partially restore the Temple and to sit in it, proclaiming that he is God-the Christ-Jesus Christ-the Messiah.

> 2 Th 2:3 ¶ *Let no man deceive you by any means: for that day shall not come, except there come a falling away first, and that man of sin be revealed, the son of perdition;*
> 2 Th 2:4 *Who opposeth and exalteth himself above all that is called God, or that is worshipped; <u>so that he as God sitteth in the temple of God, shewing himself that he is God.</u>*

With the two witnesses having been killed earlier, the Antichrist sits in the Holy Temple and directs the war against those still believing in the real God and the real Jesus Christ. The False Prophet (the Pope) relocates from the Vatican, and assists the Antichrist, seeking for all to do homage to the Antichrist. According to these verses above, the Antichrist sits in the temple of God, in Jerusalem. According to Rev 13:14 the Antichrist also has a statue of himself placed in the temple.

Rev 13:14 *And deceiveth them that dwell on the earth by the means of those miracles which he had power to do in the sight of the beast; saying to them that dwell on the earth, that they should make an image to the beast, which had the wound by a sword, and did live.*
Rev 13:15 *And he had power to give life unto the image of the beast, that the image of the beast should both speak, and cause that as many as would not worship the image of the beast should be killed.*
Rev 13:16 *And he causeth all, both small and great, rich and poor, free and bond, to receive a mark in their right hand, or in their foreheads:*
Rev 13:17 *And that no man might buy or sell, save he that had the mark, or the name of the beast, or the number of his name.*
Rev 13:18 *Here is wisdom. Let him that hath understanding count the number of the beast: for it is the number of a man; and his number is Six hundred threescore and six.*

From my previous book "Understanding the Book of Revelation", the notes for Rev 13:15-18 are:

Notes for 13:15 The False Prophet causes the statue of the Antichrist to talk, and those who would not worship the statue to be killed. If you think this impossible, look at the heresy trials of the past, E.G.: the inquisitions, where people, thinking they were doing God service, committed all kinds of atrocious acts. See Rev 3:21-God's instructions to the end time church of Laodicea. Note that Jesus overcame by His death. Read stories of the abomination of desolation committed by Antiochus IV, Epiphanes, (168 BC) when after conquering Jerusalem, he tried to force everyone to worship Greek gods, desecrated the Jerusalem Temple with swine blood (Endnote 8). Later he placed a statue of his god (Jupiter-Olympus-Zeus) in the Temple, and offering was made to it, and he himself later claimed to be that god. Much of this is also recorded in the books of 1 and 2 Maccabees, in the Apocrypha, and in several other historical texts.

> Revelation 3:21 *To him that overcometh will I grant to sit with me in my throne, even as I also overcame, and am set down with my Father in his throne.*

Notes for 13:16 The False Prophet causes all to receive a mark in their right hand or in their foreheads (or be killed). This is the hour of temptation spoken of (Rev 3:10). Note, the two witnesses and those that had initially believed and followed their example, will already have been killed by the Antichrist's forces before this time.

Notes for 13:17 Nobody may buy or sell, unless he had the mark, the name of the beast, or the number of his name.

Notes for 13:18 The number of the beast is 666.

The Bible is very clear in Exodus chapter 20, also known as the Ten Commandments, that we are not to make images to worship. Obviously, the Jews know this very clearly. All Christians should remember and heed this also.

> Ex 20:1 *And God spake all these words, saying,*
> Ex 20:2 *I am the LORD thy God, which have brought thee out of the land of Egypt, out of the house of bondage.*
> Ex 20:3 *Thou shalt have no other gods before me.*
> Ex 20:4 *Thou shalt not make unto thee any graven image, or any likeness of any thing that is in heaven above, or that is in the earth beneath, or that is in the water under the earth:*

Ex 20:5 *<u>Thou shalt not bow down thyself to them, nor serve them</u>: for I the LORD thy God am a jealous God, visiting the iniquity of the fathers upon the children unto the third and fourth generation of them that hate me;*

CHAPTER SEVEN

The Tribulation Martyrs

The Antichrist and his followers will eventually kill one third of mankind,

> Rev 9:18 *By these three was the third part of men killed, by the fire, and by the smoke, and by the brimstone, which issued out of their mouths.*

This one third of mankind that the Antichrist will eventually cause to be physically killed are martyrs that will refuse to worship or obey or submit to him. There will be a great influx into the Kingdom of God during the reign of the Antichrist, just as there was a great influx into the Kingdom of God during the time of the persecutions of the early Church.

> Zech 13:7 ¶ *Awake, O sword, against my shepherd, and against the man that is my fellow, saith the LORD of hosts: smite the shepherd, and the sheep shall be scattered: and I will turn mine hand upon the little ones.*
> Zech 13:8 *And it shall come to pass, that in all the land, saith the LORD, two parts therein shall be cut off and die; but the third shall be left therein.*
> Zech 13:9 *And I will bring the third part through the fire, and will refine them as silver is refined, and will try them as gold is tried:*

they shall call on my name, and I will hear them: I will say, It is my people: and they shall say, The LORD is my God.

Here, in Zech 13:7, the shepherd represents the two witnesses, the Apostles and Prophets of God, that are killed in accordance with the will of God, just as the Great Shepherd and Apostle and Prophet-Jesus Christ-was killed in accordance with the will of God. Just as Jesus' death and resurrection was to bring many to God, as the notes for Rev 11: 11-12 above explain, the death and resurrection of the two witnesses will bring many to God.

Just as after the death and resurrection of Jesus Christ, His followers were persecuted and killed in accordance with the will of God, so also will the little ones, meaning the followers of the Apostles and Prophets, be persecuted and killed in accordance with the will of God (by Satanic forces).

The Lord considers the death of His saints as precious:

Psalm 116:15 *Precious in the sight of the LORD is the death of his saints.*

The two thirds of mankind that shall be cut off and die (Zech 13:8) are the ungodly who will be cut off spiritually and die spiritually. These do not continue to resist the Antichrist. The other one third of mankind will be brought through the fires of persecution, lack, and martyrdom to be refined as gold-the most precious metal of Zechariah's time, and God will say of them: "It is My people".

The rest of mankind (the two thirds) that are not killed physically by the Antichrist's forces do not repent of their sins or allegiance to the Antichrist, because the Antichrist's forces are not asking or compelling them to do so:

Rev 9:20 *And the rest of the men which were not killed by these plagues yet repented not of the works of their hands, that they should not worship devils, and idols of gold, and silver, and brass, and stone, and of wood: which neither can see, nor hear, nor walk:*

Rev 9:21 *Neither repented they of their murders, nor of their sorceries, nor of their fornication, nor of their thefts.*

With the Antichrist and his False Prophet (the Pope) in full control of the Earth, they require the allegiance of every person, or they will be put to death.

Rev 13:14 *And deceiveth them that dwell on the earth by the means of those miracles which he had power to do in the sight of the beast; saying to them that dwell on the earth, that they should make an image to the beast, which had the wound by a sword, and did live.*
Rev 13:15 *And he had power to give life unto the image of the beast, that the image of the beast should both speak, and cause that as many as would not worship the image of the beast should be killed.*
Rev 13:16 *And he causeth all, both small and great, rich and poor, free and bond, to receive a mark in their right hand, or in their foreheads:*
Rev 13:17 *And that no man might buy or sell, save he that had the mark, or the name of the beast, or the number of his name.*
Rev 13:18 *Here is wisdom. Let him that hath understanding count the number of the beast: for it is the number of a man; and his number is Six hundred threescore and six.*

There will be a great many martyrs for the real Jesus Christ who will not follow the Antichrist or the False Prophet/Pope. This is called the First Reaping (verses 13-16 below).

Rev 14:6 ¶ *And I saw another angel fly in the midst of heaven, having the everlasting gospel to preach unto them that dwell on the earth, and to every nation, and kindred, and tongue, and people,*
Rev 14:7 *Saying with a loud voice, Fear God, and give glory to him; for the hour of his judgment is come: and worship him that made heaven, and earth, and the sea, and the fountains of waters.*

Rev 14:8 *And there followed another angel, saying, Babylon is fallen, is fallen, that great city, because she made all nations drink of the wine of the wrath of her fornication.*

Rev 14:9 *And the third angel followed them, saying with a loud voice, If any man worship the beast and his image, and receive his mark in his forehead, or in his hand,*

Rev 14:10 *The same shall drink of the wine of the wrath of God, which is poured out without mixture into the cup of his indignation; and he shall be tormented with fire and brimstone in the presence of the holy angels, and in the presence of the Lamb:*

Rev 14:11 *And the smoke of their torment ascendeth up for ever and ever: and they have no rest day nor night, who worship the beast and his image, and whosoever receiveth the mark of his name.*

Rev 14:12 *Here is the patience of the saints: here are they that keep the commandments of God, and the faith of Jesus.*

Rev 14:13 ¶ *And I heard a voice from heaven saying unto me, Write, Blessed are the dead which die in the Lord from henceforth: Yea, saith the Spirit, that they may rest from their labours; and their works do follow them.*

Rev 14:14 *And I looked, and behold a white cloud, and upon the cloud one sat like unto the Son of man, having on his head a golden crown, and in his hand a sharp sickle.*

Rev 14:15 *And another angel came out of the temple, crying with a loud voice to him that sat on the cloud, Thrust in thy sickle, and reap: for the time is come for thee to reap; for the harvest of the earth is ripe.*

Rev 14:16 *And he that sat on the cloud thrust in his sickle on the earth; and the earth was reaped.*

There story is also told in Rev 7:9-15:

Rev 7:9 *After this I beheld, and, lo, a great multitude, which no man could number, of all nations, and kindreds, and people, and tongues, stood before the throne, and before the Lamb, clothed with white robes, and palms in their hands;*

Rev 7:10 *And cried with a loud voice, saying, Salvation to our God which sitteth upon the throne, and unto the Lamb.*

Rev 7:11 *And all the angels stood round about the throne, and about the elders and the four beasts, and fell before the throne on their faces, and worshipped God,*

Rev 7:12 *Saying, Amen: Blessing, and glory, and wisdom, and thanksgiving, and honour, and power, and might, be unto our God for ever and ever. Amen.*

Rev 7:13 ¶ *And one of the elders answered, saying unto me, What are these which are arrayed in white robes? and whence came they?*

Rev 7:14 *And I said unto him, Sir, thou knowest. And he said to me, These are they which came out of great tribulation, and have washed their robes, and made them white in the blood of the Lamb.*

Rev 7:15 *Therefore are they before the throne of God, and serve him day and night in his temple: and he that sitteth on the throne shall dwell among them.*

The Roman Catholic Church has a long history of putting to death those who will not believe their way. For example, the Inquisitions of Europe, beginning about 1200 AD during the reign of Pope Innocent III, and also the many wars of Europe. Under one chief inquisitor, Torquemada, in just 18 years, "ten thousand two hundred and twenty persons were burned alive and ninety-seven thousand three hundred and twenty two punished with loss of property, or imprisonment" This was recorded by the Spanish historian of the Inquisition.(Endnote 9) When the Roman Catholic Church is in full power, independent thought and beliefs are dangerous and entire villages and groups of people are murdered for their beliefs, as evidenced by books such as Foxe's Book of Martyrs and secular history also.

The great tribulation period ends with the end of this first reaping, the gathering of the martyrs, the harvest of the Earth (Rev 14:15). It does not last until Jesus' Second Coming. The tribulation period is to try those upon the Earth, to cause people to make a decision to follow Jesus or the Antichrist.

After this first reaping, the gathering the harvest of the earth (Rev 14:15), two things happen. First, Rev 15:5-8 says that the temple in heaven is opened and the seven vials (or bowls) of God's wrath are given to seven angels, and that no man can enter the temple until these seven vials of God's wrath are completed upon the Earth.

> Rev 15:5 *And after that I looked, and, behold, the temple of the tabernacle of the testimony in heaven was opened:*
> Rev 15:6 *And the seven angels came out of the temple, having the seven plagues, clothed in pure and white linen, and having their breasts girded with golden girdles.*
> Rev 15:7 *And one of the four beasts gave unto the seven angels seven golden vials full of the wrath of God, who liveth for ever and ever.*
> Rev 15:8 *And the temple was filled with smoke from the glory of God, and from his power; and no man was able to enter into the temple, till the seven plagues of the seven angels were fulfilled.*

The second thing that happens after the first reaping is that the time of the Marriage Supper of the Lamb has come. This is described in Rev 19:7-9. This occurs while the wrath of God (the seven vials) is being poured out upon the Earth.

> Rev 19:7 *Let us be glad and rejoice, and give honour to him: for the marriage of the Lamb is come, and his wife hath made herself ready.*
> Rev 19:8 *And to her was granted that she should be arrayed in fine linen, clean and white: for the fine linen is the righteousness of saints.*
> Rev 19:9 *And he saith unto me, Write, Blessed are they which are called unto the marriage supper of the Lamb. And he saith unto me, These are the true sayings of God.*

These people that are called to the Marriage Supper of the Lamb are called blessed, and they are given white linen robe of righteousness. From

my previous book Understanding the Book of Revelation, the notes for
Rev 19:9 are:

> Notes for Rev 19:9 "Blessed are they which are called to the
> Marriage Supper of the Lamb of God, because they are already
> declared righteous. The "tribulation" period is over before the
> battle of Armageddon at Jesus' Second Coming. This tribulation
> period is a time of great testing, forcing people to make a choice
> and act accordingly. The tribulation is for those who will overcome
> and make it to heaven during that period. The tribulation period
> does not include the subsequent time, which is when those who
> reject Jesus will suffer God's wrath. The tribulation period ends
> with the martyrs in Heaven, and any new human entry into the
> temple in Heaven is prohibited, because the Marriage Supper of
> the Lamb has begun, and only those invited (and obviously present
> at the beginning of the Marriage Supper) are allowed to enter.
>
> Also, on Earth the beginning of 7 vials/bowls (the wrath of God)
> (Re chapter 15:8) takes place.
>
> > Rev 15:8 *And the temple was filled with smoke from the
> > glory of God, and from his power; and no man was able to
> > enter into the temple, till the seven plagues of the seven
> > angels were fulfilled.* " "

Note, that there are no latecomers to the Marriage Supper. Also these,
at the Marriage Supper of the Lamb, have already been given and are
clothed in fine white clean linen. This means that they have already been
judged as righteous. Examples of white robes or white linen being a
judgment of being declared righteous or blessed are:

> Rev 6:9 ¶ *And when he had opened the fifth seal, I saw under the
> altar the souls of them that were slain for the word of God, and for
> the testimony which they held:*

Rev 6:10 An*d they cried with a loud voice, saying, How long, O Lord, holy and true, dost thou not judge and avenge our blood on them that dwell on the earth?*
Rev 6:11 *And white robes were given unto every one of them; and it was said unto them, that they should rest yet for a little season, until their fellowservants also and their brethren, that should be killed as they were, should be fulfilled.*

Re 3:5 He *that overcometh, the same shall be clothed in* <u>white</u> *raiment; and I will not blot out his name out of the book of life, but I will confess his name before my Father, and before his angels.*

Re 7:9 *After this I beheld, and, lo, a great multitude, which no man could number, of all nations, and kindreds, and people, and tongues, stood before the throne, and before the Lamb, clothed with* <u>white</u> *robes, and palms in their hands;*

Re 7:13 *And one of the elders answered, saying unto me, What are these which are arrayed in* <u>white</u> *robes? and whence came they?*
Re 7:14 *And I said unto him, Sir, thou knowest. And he said to me, These are they which came out of great tribulation, and have washed their robes, and made them* <u>white</u> *in the blood of the Lamb*

Re 19:8 *And to her was granted that she should be arrayed in fine linen, clean and* <u>white</u>*: for the fine linen is the righteousness of saints..*

Sometime after the False Prophet/Pope relocates to the Temple in Jerusalem, judgment will come to the Vatican. God will cause the ten nation confederacy to destroy the Vatican.

Rev 17:12 *And the ten horns which thou sawest are ten kings, which have received no kingdom as yet; but receive power as kings one hour with the beast.*

Rev 17:13 *These have one mind, and shall give their power and strength unto the beast.*

Rev 17:14 *These shall make war with the Lamb, and the Lamb shall overcome them: for he is Lord of lords, and King of kings: and they that are with him are called, and chosen, and faithful.*

Rev 17:15 *And he saith unto me, The waters which thou sawest, where the whore sitteth, are peoples, and multitudes, and nations, and tongues.*

Rev 17:16 *And the ten horns which thou sawest upon the beast, these shall hate the whore, and shall make her desolate and naked, and shall eat her flesh, and burn her with fire.*

Rev 18:4 *And I heard another voice from heaven, saying, Come out of her, my people, that ye be not partakers of her sins, and that ye receive not of her plagues.*

Rev 18:5 *For her sins have reached unto heaven, and God hath remembered her iniquities.*

Rev 18:6 *Reward her even as she rewarded you, and double unto her double according to her works: in the cup which she hath filled fill to her double.*

Rev 18:7 *How much she hath glorified herself, and lived deliciously, so much torment and sorrow give her: for she saith in her heart, I sit a queen, and am no widow, and shall see no sorrow.*

Rev 18:8 *Therefore shall her plagues come in one day, death, and mourning, and famine; and she shall be utterly burned with fire: for strong is the Lord God who judgeth her.*

Rev 18:9 *¶ And the kings of the earth, who have committed fornication and lived deliciously with her, shall bewail her, and lament for her, when they shall see the smoke of her burning,*

Rev 18:10 *Standing afar off for the fear of her torment, saying, Alas, alas, that great city Babylon, that mighty city! for in one hour is thy judgment come.*

Rev 18:21 *And a mighty angel took up a stone like a great millstone, and cast it into the sea, saying, Thus with violence shall that great city Babylon be thrown down, and shall be found no more at all*

The notes from my previous book Understanding the Book of Revelation for verses 10 and 21 are:

Notes for 18:10 "This is describing the destruction of the city of Rome and the Vatican. This is by nuclear explosion(s), which will be caused by the forces of the Antichrist. Nuclear weapon(s) will be used to ensure that the underground areas of the Vatican are completely destroyed also. People stand afar off for fear of the nuclear radiation caused by the blast(s). In one hour she was destroyed completely."

Notes for Rev 18:21: "This mighty angel demonstrates how her destruction shall be. It shall be accomplished quickly and violently. It shall come from the sky. There shall be no defense or resistance against it. This place shall be completely obliterated. The destruction shall be complete."

CHAPTER EIGHT

Jesus' Second Coming
and
The Seventh Trumpet

On Earth, before Jesus' Second Coming another process will happen while the Marriage Supper of the Lamb is going on in Heaven. Included in the seven vials is the 6th vial, Rev 16:12-16. The armies of the Kings of the East shall advance towards the Euphrates River, and onward to Israel and Jerusalem. This takes time, but they will eventually gather at Armageddon to fight against Jesus when He comes. The gathering of the armies of the Kings of the East is not to do battle against the western world or against each other, but to do battle against Jesus.

Earlier, it was shown beginning in Rev 9:13, that the 6th trumpet was the beginning of the Antichrist's 3 ½ years of unlimited power on the Earth, including the power to kill anybody.

> Rev 9:13 ¶ *And the sixth angel sounded, and I heard a voice from the four horns of the golden altar which is before God,*
> Rev 9:14 *Saying to the sixth angel which had the trumpet, Loose the four angels which are bound in the great river Euphrates.*
> Rev 9:15 *And the four angels were loosed, which were prepared for an hour, and a day, and a month, and a year, for to slay the third part of men.*

Rev 9:16 And the number of the army of the horsemen were two hundred thousand thousand: and I heard the number of them.

Now at this time, this has progressed to the point as described in Rev 16:12-16.

Rev 16:12 ¶ And the sixth angel poured out his vial upon the great river Euphrates; and the water thereof was dried up, that the way of the kings of the east might be prepared.

Rev 16:13 And I saw three unclean spirits like frogs come out of the mouth of the dragon, and out of the mouth of the beast, and out of the mouth of the false prophet.

Rev 16:14 For they are the spirits of devils, working miracles, which go forth unto the kings of the earth and of the whole world, to gather them to the battle of that great day of God Almighty.

Rev 16:15 Behold, I come as a thief. Blessed is he that watcheth, and keepeth his garments, lest he walk naked, and they see his shame.

Rev 16:16 And he gathered them together into a place called in the Hebrew tongue Armageddon.

In Heaven, the Marriage Supper of the Lamb is followed by the assembling of the armies of Heaven that will come down to Earth with Jesus Christ at His Second Coming.

Rev 19:11 ¶ And I saw heaven opened, and behold a white horse; and he that sat upon him was called Faithful and True, and in righteousness he doth judge and make war.

Rev 19:12 His eyes were as a flame of fire, and on his head were many crowns; and he had a name written, that no man knew, but he himself.

Rev 19:13 And he was clothed with a vesture dipped in blood: and his name is called The Word of God.

Rev 19:14 And the armies which were in heaven followed him upon white horses, clothed in fine linen, white and clean.

Rev 19:15 *And out of his mouth goeth a sharp sword, that with it he should smite the nations: and he shall rule them with a rod of iron: and he treadeth the winepress of the fierceness and wrath of Almighty God.*
Rev 19:16 *And he hath on his vesture and on his thigh a name written, KING OF KINGS, AND LORD OF LORDS.*

As seen in verse 14 above, those people coming back with Jesus (Rev 19:14) are already clothed in fine white clean linen. As explained in the last chapter, this means that they have already been judged as righteous.

Jesus Christ is not coming this time as the meek Lamb of God, but as a Man of war, as the King of Kings and Lord of Lords. He is coming in the clouds with great power and glory and to execute judgment and vengeance upon the ungodly of the Earth. The whole world will see Him. There will be a great slaughter of the ungodly

Mat 24: 30 *And then shall appear the sign of the Son of man in heaven: and then shall all the tribes of the earth mourn, and they shall see the Son of man coming in the clouds of heaven with power and great glory.*

Quite possibly the "sign of the Son of man" appearing in heaven will be an extremely large cross seen in Heaven. The cross seems to be almost universally identified with Jesus.

This completes the mystery of God. As explained in my previous book Understanding the Book of Revelation, in the notes for Rev 10:7:

Notes for Rev 10:7 "but when the seventh angel sounds his trumpet (the SEVENTH TRUMPET, also called the THIRD WOE), the mystery of God should be finished (as He has told His prophets). This will be the opening of the heavens and the visual revelation of Christ to the people of Earth (Mark 13:26 & Rev 6:14). It is no longer a mystery to the people of Earth."

Mark 13:26 *And then shall they see the Son of man coming in the clouds with great power and glory.*

Revelation 6:14 *And the heaven departed as a scroll when it is rolled together; and every mountain and island were moved out of their places.*

From the Bible, the **SEVENTH TRUMPET**:

Rev 10:5 *And the angel which I saw stand upon the sea and upon the earth lifted up his hand to heaven,*
Rev 10:6 *And sware by him that liveth for ever and ever, who created heaven, and the things that therein are, and the earth, and the things that therein are, and the sea, and the things which are therein, that there should be time no longer:*
Rev 10:7 *But in the days of the voice of the seventh angel, when he shall begin to sound, the mystery of God should be finished, as he hath declared to his servants the prophets.*

When the "sign of the son of man" and Jesus Christ Himself and the armies of Heaven are seen in Heaven coming to the Earth, there is no longer any mystery about it, but the whole world will see it. Jesus will come back to the Mount of Olives, just east of Jerusalem, where He left the Earth before. He will come to fight against the forces of the Antichrist, and there will be a great slaughter of the ungodly which attempt to fight against Jesus.

The story, as told by the prophet Joel:

Joel 3:12 *Let the heathen be wakened, and come up to the valley of Jehoshaphat: for there will I sit to judge all the heathen round about.*
Joel 3:13 *Put ye in the sickle, for the harvest is ripe: come, get you down; for the press is full, the fats overflow; for their wickedness is great.*
Joel 3:14 *Multitudes, multitudes in the valley of decision: for the day of the LORD is near in the valley of decision.*

Joel 3:15 *The sun and the moon shall be darkened, and the stars shall withdraw their shining.*
Joel 3:16 *The LORD also shall roar out of Zion, and utter his voice from Jerusalem; and the heavens and the earth shall shake: but the LORD will be the hope of his people, and the strength of the children of Israel.*

The story, as explained in Revelation chapter 19:

Rev 19:13 *And he was clothed with a vesture dipped in blood: and his name is called The Word of God.*
Rev 19:14 *And the armies which were in heaven followed him upon white horses, clothed in fine linen, white and clean.*
Rev 19:15 *And out of his mouth goeth a sharp sword, that with it he should smite the nations: and he shall rule them with a rod of iron: and he treadeth the winepress of the fierceness and wrath of Almighty God.*
Rev 19:16 *And he hath on his vesture and on his thigh a name written, KING OF KINGS, AND LORD OF LORDS.*
Rev 19:17 *And I saw an angel standing in the sun; and he cried with a loud voice, saying to all the fowls that fly in the midst of heaven, Come and gather yourselves together unto the supper of the great God;*
Rev 19:18 *That ye may eat the flesh of kings, and the flesh of captains, and the flesh of mighty men, and the flesh of horses, and of them that sit on them, and the flesh of all men, both free and bond, both small and great.*
Rev 19:19 *And I saw the beast, and the kings of the earth, and their armies, gathered together to make war against him that sat on the horse, and against his army.*
Rev 19:20 *And the beast was taken, and with him the false prophet that wrought miracles before him, with which he deceived them that had received the mark of the beast, and them that worshipped*

*his image. These both were cast alive into a lake of fire burning
with brimstone.*

*Rev 19:21 And the remnant were slain with the sword of him that
sat upon the horse, which sword proceeded out of his mouth: and
all the fowls were filled with their flesh.*

The story as told by Zechariah:

*Zech 14:3 Then shall the LORD go forth, and fight against those
nations, as when he fought in the day of battle.*

*Zech 14:4 And his feet shall stand in that day upon the mount of
Olives, which is before Jerusalem on the east, and the mount of Olives
shall cleave in the midst thereof toward the east and toward the west,
and there shall be a very great valley; and half of the mountain shall
remove toward the north, and half of it toward the south.*

*Zech 14:5 And ye shall flee to the valley of the mountains; for the
valley of the mountains shall reach unto Azal: yea, ye shall flee,
like as ye fled from before the earthquake in the days of Uzziah
king of Judah: and the LORD my God shall come, and all the
saints with thee.*

*Zech 14:6 And it shall come to pass in that day, that the light shall
not be clear, nor dark:*

As Zechariah prophesied above in Zech 14:4, Jesus returns to Earth at
the very place where He left it, at the Mount of Olives:

*Acts 1:9 And when he had spoken these things, while they beheld,
he was taken up; and a cloud received him out of their sight.*

*Acts 1:10 And while they looked stedfastly toward heaven as he
went up, behold, two men stood by them in white apparel;*

*Acts 1:11 Which also said, Ye men of Galilee, why stand ye gazing up
into heaven? this same Jesus, which is taken up from you into heaven,
shall so come in like manner as ye have seen him go into heaven.*

Acts 1:*12* ¶ *Then returned they unto Jerusalem from the mount called Olivet, which is from Jerusalem a sabbath day's journey.*

Thomas Velez

CHAPTER NINE

Jesus Reigns

After Jesus takes control of the Earth by destroying those that gathered against Him, Jesus will reign here on the Earth for 1,000 years.

As For The Nation Of Israel
Jerusalem shall be safely inhabited and Jesus the Messiah shall dwell in and rule from Zion, the holy mountain of God, and Jerusalem shall be holy. Zechariah chapter 14 says:

> Zech 14:8 ¶ *And it shall be in that day, that living waters shall go out from Jerusalem; half of them toward the former sea, and half of them toward the hinder sea: in summer and in winter shall it be.*
> Zech 14:9 *And the LORD shall be king over all the earth: in that day shall there be one LORD, and his name one.*
> Zech 14:10 *All the land shall be turned as a plain from Geba to Rimmon south of Jerusalem: and it shall be lifted up, and inhabited in her place, from Benjamin's gate unto the place of the first gate, unto the corner gate, and from the tower of Hananeel unto the king's winepresses.*
> Zech 14:11 *And men shall dwell in it, and there shall be no more utter destruction; but Jerusalem shall be safely inhabited.*

The story as told by the prophet Joel:

Joel 3:17 *So shall ye know that I am the LORD your God dwelling in Zion, my holy mountain: then shall Jerusalem be holy, and there shall no strangers pass through her any more.*

Joel 3:18 ¶ *And it shall come to pass in that day, that the mountains shall drop down new wine, and the hills shall flow with milk, and all the rivers of Judah shall flow with waters, and a fountain shall come forth of the house of the LORD, and shall water the valley of Shittim.*

Joel 3:19 *Egypt shall be a desolation, and Edom shall be a desolate wilderness, for the violence against the children of Judah, because they have shed innocent blood in their land.*

Joel 3:20 *But Judah shall dwell for ever, and Jerusalem from generation to generation.*

Joel 3:21 *For I will cleanse their blood that I have not cleansed: for the LORD dwelleth in Zion.*

As For Those In The First Resurrection

Revelation chapter 20 says they shall reign with Christ:

Rev 20:4 *And I saw thrones, and they sat upon them, and judgment was given unto them: and I saw the souls of them that were beheaded for the witness of Jesus, and for the word of God, and which had not worshipped the beast, neither his image, neither had received his mark upon their foreheads, or in their hands; and they lived and reigned with Christ a thousand years.*

Rev 20:5 *But the rest of the dead lived not again until the thousand years were finished. This is the first resurrection.*

Rev 20:6 *Blessed and holy is he that hath part in the first resurrection: on such the second death hath no power, but they shall be priests of God and of Christ, and shall reign with him a thousand years.*

As For The Remainder Of The Peoples Of The Nations Of The Earth

Zechariah chapter14 says:

Zech 14:16 *And it shall come to pass, that every one that is left of all the nations which came against Jerusalem shall even go up from year to year to worship the King, the LORD of hosts, and to keep the feast of tabernacles.*

Zech 14:17 *And it shall be, that whoso will not come up of all the families of the earth unto Jerusalem to worship the King, the LORD of hosts, even upon them shall be no rain.*

Zech 14:18 *And if the family of Egypt go not up, and come not, that have no rain; there shall be the plague, wherewith the LORD will smite the heathen that come not up to keep the feast of tabernacles.*

Zech 14:19 *This shall be the punishment of Egypt, and the punishment of all nations that come not up to keep the feast of tabernacles.*

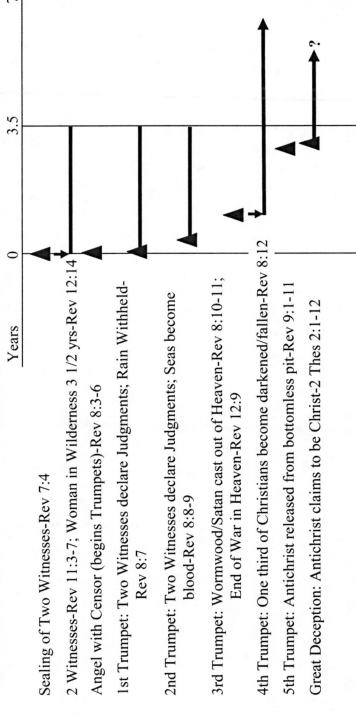

Schedule Part 1 of 2-Not to Scale-Dates Approximate-Last 7 years before Jesus' Second Coming

Years

0   3.5   7

Sealing of Two Witnesses-Rev 7:4

2 Witnesses-Rev 11:3-7; Woman in Wilderness 3 1/2 yrs-Rev 12:14

Angel with Censor (begins Trumpets)-Rev 8:3-6

1st Trumpet: Two Witnesses declare Judgments; Rain Withheld-
      Rev 8:7

2nd Trumpet: Two Witnesses declare Judgments; Seas become
      blood-Rev 8:8-9

3rd Trumpet: Wormwood/Satan cast out of Heaven-Rev 8:10-11;
      End of War in Heaven-Rev 12:9

4th Trumpet: One third of Christians become darkened/fallen-Rev 8:12

5th Trumpet: Antichrist released from bottomless pit-Rev 9:1-11

Great Deception: Antichrist claims to be Christ-2 Thes 2:1-12

Thomas Velez

Schedule Part 2 of 2-Not to Scale-Dates Approximate-Last 7 years before Jesus' Second Coming

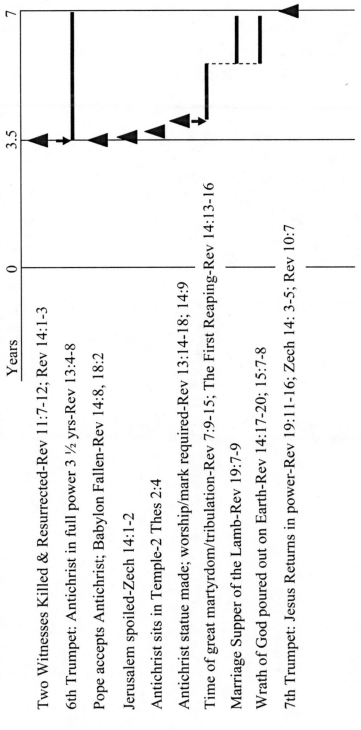

Years

Two Witnesses Killed & Resurrected-Rev 11:7-12; Rev 14:1-3

6th Trumpet: Antichrist in full power 3 ½ yrs-Rev 13:4-8

Pope accepts Antichrist; Babylon Fallen-Rev 14:8, 18:2

Jerusalem spoiled-Zech 14:1-2

Antichrist sits in Temple-2 Thes 2:4

Antichrist statue made; worship/mark required-Rev 13:14-18; 14:9

Time of great martyrdom/tribulation-Rev 7:9-15; The First Reaping-Rev 14:13-16

Marriage Supper of the Lamb-Rev 19:7-9

Wrath of God poured out on Earth-Rev 14:17-20; 15:7-8

7th Trumpet: Jesus Returns in power-Rev 19:11-16; Zech 14: 3-5; Rev 10:7

Thomas Velez

CHAPTER TEN

Salvation

There is only one way to God and Heaven:

1 Tim 2:5 *For there is one God, and one mediator between God and men, the man Christ Jesus;*

John 14:6 *Jesus saith unto him, I am the way, the truth, and the life: no man cometh unto the Father, but by me.*

All have sinned:

Rom 3:10 *As it is written, There is none righteous, no, not one:*

Rom 3:23 *For all have sinned, and come short of the glory of God;*

The punishment for sins is spiritual "death" which is condemnation to the lake of fire/hell where the ungodly will suffer forever.

Rom 6:23 *For the wages of sin is death; but the gift of God is eternal life through Jesus Christ our Lord.*

Mat 25:41 *Then shall he say also unto them on the left hand, Depart from me, ye cursed, into everlasting fire, prepared for the devil and his angels:*

Mat 25:42 *For I was an hungred, and ye gave me no meat: I was thirsty, and ye gave me no drink:*

Mat 25:43 *I was a stranger, and ye took me not in: naked, and ye clothed me not: sick, and in prison, and ye visited me not.*

Mat 25:44 *Then shall they also answer him, saying, Lord, when saw we thee an hungred, or athirst, or a stranger, or naked, or sick, or in prison, and did not minister unto thee?*

Mat 25:45 *Then shall he answer them, saying, Verily I say unto you, Inasmuch as ye did it not to one of the least of these, ye did it not to me.*

Mat 25:46 *And these shall go away into everlasting punishment: but the righteous into life eternal.*

Mark 9:43 *And if thy hand offend thee, cut it off: it is better for thee to enter into life maimed, than having two hands to go into hell, into the fire that never shall be quenched:*

Mark 9:44 *Where their worm dieth not, and the fire is not quenched.*

We need a savior, we cannot earn our salvation, but God loved us so much He made a way for us by sending Jesus, and Jesus died willingly for us:

John 3:16 *For God so loved the world, that he gave his only begotten Son, that whosoever believeth in him should not perish, but have everlasting life.*

John 3: 17 *For God sent not his Son into the world to condemn the world; but that the world through him might be saved.*

John 3:18 *He that believeth on him is not condemned: but he that believeth not is condemned already, because he hath not believed in the name of the only begotten Son of God.*

Eph 2:8 *For by grace are ye saved through faith; and that not of yourselves: it is the gift of God:*

Eph 2:9 *Not of works, lest any man should boast.*

Who can be saved:

Rom 10:13 *For whosoever shall call upon the name of the Lord shall be saved.*

How to get saved:

Rom 10:9 *That if thou shalt confess with thy mouth the Lord Jesus, and shalt believe in thine heart that God hath raised him from the dead, thou shalt be saved.*
Rom 10:10 *For with the heart man believeth unto righteousness; and with the mouth confession is made unto salvation.*

If you freely choose to be saved, believe and say something like this:

Jesus, I believe you are the Son of God and died for my sins. I believe that God raised you from the dead. I ask you to forgive me of my past and come into my life forever. Save me and help me. I love you. Amen.

If you believed and did that, you can be assured that you have eternal life.

1 John 5:12 *He that hath the Son hath life; and he that hath not the Son of God hath not life.*
1 John 5:13 *These things have I written unto you that believe on the name of the Son of God; that ye may know that ye have eternal life, and that ye may believe on the name of the Son of God.*

Then:

1. Go tell someone that you accepted Jesus as your savior.

2. Begin to read a Bible every day if possible. A good place to begin is in John or Matthew.

3. Find a good Bible believing Church and that also believes in the gifts of the Spirit as described in 1 Corinthians chapter 12:7-11, including the gift of speaking in tongues, and attend it regularly.

4. After you have made the choice to receive Jesus as your savior, get baptized in water, by immersion into the water, like Jesus did.

5. Ask someone you trust that has the "Baptism of the Holy Ghost" and speaks in tongues, to lead you into that also. If you know of nobody that does, ask God directly to baptize you in the Holy Ghost with the evidence of speaking in tongues.

Appendix I

Scriptures Wrongly Interpreted to be a Pre-Tribulation Rapture and Other Scriptures

A) 1 Thessalonians chapter 4:

> 1 Thes 4:13 ¶ *But I would not have you to be ignorant, brethren, concerning them which are asleep, that ye sorrow not, even as others which have no hope.*
> 1 Thes 4:14 *For if we believe that Jesus died and rose again, even so them also which sleep in Jesus will God bring with him.*
> 1 Thes 4:15 *For this we say unto you by the word of the Lord, that we which are alive and remain unto the coming of the Lord shall not prevent them which are asleep.*
> 1 Thes 4:16 *For the Lord himself shall descend from heaven with a shout, with the voice of the archangel, and with the trump of God: and the dead in Christ shall rise first:*

1 Thes 4:17 *Then we which are alive and remain shall be caught up together with them in the clouds, to meet the Lord in the air: and so shall we ever be with the Lord.*

Note: the resurrection of the dead occurs before the rapture!!! When is the resurrection of the dead? Rev 20 tells us.

Rev 20:11 ¶ *And I saw a great white throne, and him that sat on it, from whose face the earth and the heaven fled away; and there was found no place for them.*

Rev 20:12 *And I saw the dead, small and great, stand before God; and the books were opened: and another book was opened, which is the book of life: and the dead were judged out of those things which were written in the books, according to their works.*

Rev 20:13 *And the sea gave up the dead which were in it; and death and hell delivered up the dead which were in them: and they were judged every man according to their works.*

Rev 20:14 *And death and hell were cast into the lake of fire. This is the second death.*

Rev 20:15 *And whosoever was not found written in the book of life was cast into the lake of fire.*

Rev 21:1 ¶ *And I saw a new heaven and a new earth: for the first heaven and the first earth were passed away; and there was no more sea.*

Note: the resurrection of the dead occurs just before the great white throne judgment of God, at the end of this world, just before the creation of the New Heaven and the New Earth.

B) 1 Corinthians chapter 15:

1 Cor 15:12 ¶ *Now if Christ be preached that he rose from the dead, how say some among you that there is no* **resurrection of the dead***?*

Note: The subject is the resurrection of the dead!!!

1 Cor 15:20 *But now is Christ risen from the dead, and become the firstfruits of them that slept.*
1 Cor 15:21 *For since by man came death, by man came also the resurrection of the dead.*
1 Cor 15:22 *For as in Adam all die, even so in Christ shall all be made alive.*
1 Cor 15:23 *But every man in his own order: Christ the firstfruits; afterward they that are Christ's at his coming*
1 Cor 15:24 *Then cometh the end, when he shall have delivered up the kingdom to God, even the Father; when he shall have put down all rule and all authority and power.*
1 Cor 15:25 *For he must reign, till he hath put all enemies under his feet.*
1 Cor 15:26 **The last enemy that shall be destroyed is death***.*

Note: Verse 26 says the last enemy destroyed is death. There are no more enemies after death is conquered. There are no more deaths.

1 Cor 15:42 *So also is the* **resurrection of the dead***. It is sown in corruption; it is raised in incorruption:*

1 Cor 15:50 *Now this I say, brethren, that* **flesh and blood cannot inherit the kingdom of God***; neither doth corruption inherit incorruption.*
1 Cor 15:51 ¶ *Behold, I shew you a mystery; We shall not all sleep, but we shall all be changed,*

1 Cor 15:52 *In a moment, in the twinkling of an eye, **at the last trump**: for the trumpet shall sound, and **the dead shall be raised incorruptible, and we shall be changed.***

Note, this Rapture occurs at the last trump, when the dead are raised incorruptible. Note, the last trumpet cannot be before the last seven years before Jesus' Second Coming, because there are many trumpets blown during the last seven years in the Book of Revelation.

1 Cor 15:53 *For this corruptible must put on incorruption, and this mortal must put on immortality.*
1 Cor 15:54 *So when this corruptible shall have put on incorruption, and this mortal shall have put on immortality, then shall be brought to pass the saying that is written, Death is swallowed up in victory.*

Verse 26 said: **The last enemy *that* shall be destroyed *is* death**. This also has to be after the deaths of the many Christian martyrs occurring during the last seven years before Christ's Second Coming, described many places in the Book of Revelation. Since the Rapture is after "death" is destroyed (no more deaths) and there are many Christian deaths during the last 7 years before the Second Coming, there cannot be a Pre-Tribulation Rapture.

C) Explanation for 2 Thes 2:7

This scripture is used by some to prove that the Holy Spirit in people is what restrains the Antichrist, and that the Antichrist cannot come until the Holy Spirit is removed from the Earth. This philosophy has many problems.

- There is not one Biblical reference about the Holy Spirit being removed from the Earth. It is the job of the Holy Spirit to draw men to Jesus and to comfort and lead Christians, INCLUDING during the tribulation period.

• If the Holy Spirit is removed from the Earth by a Pre-Tribulation Rapture of worthy Christians, does that mean that the remaining Christians do not have, or will lose, the Holy Spirit? Of course not.

• Also, there will be many who will see the truth and will become Christian and be martyred during the tribulation period. Do they not get the Holy Spirit? Of course they will get the Holy Spirit.

Let us look at 2 Thessalonians more carefully. The names in parenthesis ( ) are my explanations of the pronouns used in the following verses.

2 Th 2:1 ¶ *Now we beseech you, brethren, by the coming of our Lord Jesus Christ, and by our gathering together unto him* (Jesus Christ),

2 Th 2:2 *That ye be not soon shaken in mind, or be troubled, neither by spirit, nor by word, nor by letter as from us, as that the day of Christ is at hand.*

2 Th 2:3 ¶ *Let no man deceive you by any means: for that day shall not come, except there come a falling away first, and that man of sin* (Antichrist) *be revealed, the son of perdition;*

2 Th 2:4 *Who opposeth and exalteth himself* (Antichrist) *above all that is called God, or that is worshipped; so that he* (Antichrist) *as God sitteth in the temple of God, shewing himself* (Antichrist) *that he* (Antichrist) *is God.*

2 Th 2:5 *Remember ye not, that, when I was yet with you, I told you these things?*

2 Th 2:6 *And now ye know what withholdeth that he* (Antichrist) *might be revealed in his* (Antichrist's) *time.*

2 Th 2:7 *For the mystery of iniquity doth already work: only he* (he that restrains the Antichrist/Apollyon/Abaddon in the bottomless

pit*) who now letteth will let, until he (the restrainer) be taken out of the way.*

2 Th 2:7 (New American Standard Version) *For the mystery of lawlessness is already at work; only he who now restrains will do so until he is taken out of the way.*

2 Th 2:8 *And then shall that Wicked* (Antichrist) *be revealed, whom* (Antichrist) *the Lord shall consume with the spirit of his* (Jesus Christ) *mouth, and shall destroy with the brightness of his* (Jesus Christ) *coming:*
2 Th 2:9 *Even him*(Antichrist), *whose coming is after the working of Satan with all power and signs and lying wonders,*
2 Th 2:10 *And with all deceivableness of unrighteousness in them that perish; because they received not the love of the truth, that they might be saved.*
2 Th 2:11 *And for this cause God shall send them strong delusion, that they should believe a lie:*
2 Th 2:12 *That they all might be damned who believed not the truth, but had pleasure in unrighteousness.*

Examine 2 Thes 2:7 more closely:

Amplified Version:
2 Thes 2:7 *For the mystery of lawlessness (that hidden principle of rebellion against constituted authority) is already at work in the world, [but it is] restrained only until he who restrains it is taken out of the way.*

New American Standard Version:
2 Thes 2:7 *For the mystery of lawlessness is already at work; only he who now restrains will do so until he is taken out of the way.*

New International Version:
> 2 Thes 2:7 *For the secret power of lawlessness is already at work; but the one who now holds it back will continue to do so til he is taken out of the way.*

The brackets below < > enclose the Strong's Concordance numbers for the Greek version of the words in 2 Thes 2:7. Key phrases with the Strong's Concordance explanations follow the English words/phrases translated below from the Greek.

> 2 Thes 2:7 For <1063> the mystery <3466> of iniquity <458> doth <1754> <0> already <2235> work <1754> (5731): only <3440> he who now <737> letteth <2722> (5723) *will let*, until <2193> he be taken <1096> (5638) out of <1537> the way <3319>.

HE WHO NOW <737>:
737 arti arti *ar'-tee*
from a derivative of 142 (cf 740) through the idea of suspension; TDNT-4:1106,658; adv
AV-now 24, henceforth + 575 2, hereafter + 575 2, this present 2, hitherto + 2193 2, misc 4; 36
1) just now, this moment
2) now at this time, at this very time, this moment

LETTETH <2722>:
2722 katecw katecho *kat-ekh'-o*
from 2596 and 2192; TDNT-2:829,286; v
AV-hold 3, hold fast 3, keep 2, possess 2, stay 1, take 1, have 1, make 1, misc 5; 19
1) to hold back, detain, retain
  1a) from going away
  1b) to restrain, hinder (the course or progress of)

1b1) that which hinders, Antichrist from making his appearance

    1b2) to check a ship's headway i.e. to hold or head the ship

  1c) to hold fast, keep secure, keep firm possession of

2) to get possession of, take

2b) to possess

HE BE TAKEN <1096>:

1096 ginomai ginomai *ghin'-om-ahee*

a prolongation and middle voice form of a primary verb; TDNT-1:681,117;

AV-be 255, come to pass 82, be made 69, be done 63, come 52, become 47, God forbid + 3361 15, arise 13, have 5, be fulfilled 3, be married to 3, be preferred 3, not tr 14, misc 4, vr done 2; 678

1) to become, i.e. to come into existence, begin to be, receive being

2) to become, i.e. to come to pass, happen

  2a) of events

3) to arise, appear in history, come upon the stage

  3a) of men appearing in public

4) to be made, finished

  4a) of miracles, to be performed, wrought

5) to become, be made

THE WAY <3319>

3319 mesov mesos *mes'-os*

from 3326; ; adj

AV-midst 41, among 6, from among + 1537 5, midnight + 3571 2, misc 5; 6

1) middle

2) the midst

3) in the midst of, amongst

The restrainer of the the Antichrist/Apollyon/Abaddon keeps him (Antichrist) in the bottomless pit until the time of his (Antichrist) release from it. The restrainer may be an angelic guard at the "gate" of the bottomless pit.

> Rev 9:1 *And the fifth angel sounded, and I saw a star fall from heaven unto the earth: and to him was given the key of the bottomless pit.*
> Rev 9:2 *And he opened the bottomless pit; and there arose a smoke out of the pit, as the smoke of a great furnace; and the sun and the air were darkened by reason of the smoke of the pit.*
> Rev 9:3 *And there came out of the smoke locusts upon the earth: and unto them was given power, as the scorpions of the earth have power.*
>
> Rev 9:11 *And they had a king over them, which is the angel of the bottomless pit, whose name in the Hebrew tongue is Abaddon, but in the Greek tongue hath his name Apollyon.*

D) Hebrews chapter 9 says it is appoint unto men once to die.

> Heb 9:27 *And as it is appointed unto men once to die, but after this the judgment:*

E) Jesus did not pray for any of His disciples to be taken out of the world-ever.

> John 17:15 *I pray **not that thou shouldest take them out of the world**, but that thou shouldest keep them from the evil.*
> John 17:16 *They are not of the world, even as I am not of the world.*
> John 17:17 *Sanctify them through thy truth: thy word is truth.*
> John 17:18 *As thou hast sent me into the world, even so have I also sent them into the world.*

John 17:19 *And for their sakes I sanctify myself, that they also might be sanctified through the truth.*
John 17:20 *Neither pray I for these alone, but **for them also which shall believe on me** through their word;*

F) The Seven Feasts of Israel

In the Book of Leviticus, chapter 23, the seven feasts of Israel are:

PASSOVER: verses 4-5, prophesying Jesus death and shed blood on Calvary

UNLEAVENED BREAD: verses 6-8, prophesying Jesus' sinless life

FIRSTFRUITS: verses 9-14, prophesying Jesus bodily resurrection, the first of many to come

PENTECOST: verses 15-22, prophesying the coming of the Holy Spirit

TRUMPETS: verses 23-25, prophesying the time of the calling in of the harvest (evangelism) for about 2,000 years, from Pentecost until the Second Coming of Jesus (Not Signifying the Rapture) (reference book: Charles and Frances Hunter, *Angels on Assignment,* (Kingwood, Texas; Hunter Books, c1979), pp. 87-88)

DAY OF ATONEMENT: verses 26-32, prophesying repentance or punishment

TABERNACLES: verses 33-44, prophesying Jesus' return and the millennial reign of Christ living on Earth with people, ruling from Jerusalem. The world will be in peace and in worship of Jesus as Lord.

G) In Daniel chapter 9, Daniel has the famous prophesy about the seventy weeks. Although it is common for believers of a Pre-Tribulation Rapture to insert a long delay (of approximately 2,000 years) between the 69th and the 70th week, actually all 70 weeks are consecutive with no missing or inserted time. The below is a synopsis of this. Gratitude is extended to Mr Philip Mauro who wrote "The Seventy Weeks and the Great Tribulation", from which most of this interpretation of chapter 9 of Daniel is based upon. Mr. Mauro's book is available with the Online Bible at: http://www.onlinebible.net/

> Dan 9:1 ¶ *In the first year of Darius the son of Ahasuerus, of the seed of the Medes, which was made king over the realm of the Chaldeans;*
> Dan 9:2 *In the first year of his reign I Daniel understood by books the number of the years, whereof the word of the LORD came to Jeremiah the prophet, that he would <u>accomplish seventy years in the desolations of Jerusalem.</u>*

Daniel understands, from Jeremiah 25:1-12, that Jerusalem was to be punished for 70 years, and that time was coming to a close. Then Daniel prays and intercedes to the Lord for mercy on Jerusalem and its sanctuary/temple-for the holy mountain of God (verses 3-19). The subject of chapter 9 in the book of Daniel is Jerusalem, the temple, and its fate.

> Dan 9:16 *O Lord, according to all thy righteousness, I beseech thee, <u>let thine anger and thy fury be turned away from thy city Jerusalem, thy holy mountain</u>: because for our sins, and for the iniquities of our fathers, Jerusalem and thy people are become a reproach to all that are about us.*
> Dan 9:17 *Now therefore, O our God, hear the prayer of thy servant, and his supplications, and <u>cause thy face to shine upon thy sanctuary</u> that is desolate, for the Lord's sake.*
> Dan 9:20 ¶ *And whiles I was speaking, and praying, and confessing my sin and the sin of my people Israel, and presenting*

*my supplication before the LORD my God for the holy mountain of
my God;*
Dan 9:21 *Yea, whiles I was speaking in prayer, even the man
Gabriel, … … …*
Dan 9:22 *And he informed me, and talked with me, and said, O
Daniel, I am now come forth to give thee skill and understanding.*

God sends the angel Gabriel to be sure that Daniel will understand.

Dan 9:23 *At the beginning of thy supplications the commandment
came forth, and I am come to shew thee; for thou art greatly
beloved: therefore understand the matter, and consider the vision*

History shows, and most theologians agree, that the seventy weeks of the
next verse (24) represents seventy weeks of years, or 70 weeks * 7
days/week = 490 days or actually 490 years). This means that 490 years
duration is meant. To each of the following portions of scripture, I have
added my interpretation (in parentheses and in non-italicized bold print).

Dan 9:24 *Seventy weeks*
(four hundred and ninety years)

are determined upon thy people and upon thy holy city,
(are precisely settled/established upon the Jews and Jerusalem)

to finish the transgression
**(to fill up the transgression of the Jews, especially the killing of their
Messiah, Mt 23:32),**

and to make an end of sins
(end the power of sins over mankind; a total redemption, Heb 10:12),

and to make reconciliation for iniquity
(by the atonement and reconciliation by the death of Christ),

and to bring in everlasting righteousness
(by God accepting the perfect sacrifice of Jesus establishing the Kingdom of God in righteousness, Ro 14:17),

and to seal up the vision and prophecy
(to end the Jewish prophetic visions and prophetic words through the prophets of Israel, Isa 6:10).),

and to anoint the most Holy
(to anoint/give the Holy Ghost to the most Holy temples: the hearts/spirits of Christians, to begin the building of the Church; i.e. the temple of God is within men, 2Co 6:16).

Dan 9:25 *Know therefore and understand, that from the going forth of the commandment to restore and to build Jerusalem unto the Messiah*

(The Hebrew word "Messiah" [Strong's #4899]means Anointed One. Jesus was anointed by God when he received the water baptism by John in the Jordan river.)

shall be seven weeks, and threescore and two weeks: the street shall be built again, and the wall, even in troublous times.
(shall be 7*7=49 years, and 62*7=434 years, or 49+434=483 years total).

Dan 9:26 *And after*
(Beginning sometime after)

threescore and two weeks
(the 7 weeks=49 years plus the 62 weeks = 434 years totals 483 years total, since the 62 week period came after the 7 week period. This means after the 483 years.)

shall Messiah be cut off
(Jesus crucified after the 483 years or 69 weeks. This means the Messiah will be cutoff/crucified <u>in</u> the 70th week),

but not for himself
(for the sins of people):

and the people
(Romans)

of the prince
(Titus, the son of the Roman Emperor Vespasian)

that shall come shall destroy the city and the sanctuary;
(Jerusalem and the sanctuary/Temple were destroyed in 70 AD)

and the end thereof shall be with a flood
(of Roman soldiers into the city) ,

and unto the end of the war
(the fall of Masada in 73 AD)

desolations are determined.

Dan 9:27 *And he*
(Messiah/Jesus)

shall confirm the covenant
(the new covenant/New Testament)

with many
(those who would become Christians)

for one week
(seven years):

and in the midst of the week
(that same one week/seven years)

he
(Messiah/Jesus)

shall cause the sacrifice and the oblation
(the Old Testament Jewish sacrifices in their temple)

to cease
(cease to be accepted, because of the Messiah's perfect sacrifice),

and for the overspreading of abominations
(by the Jews)

he
(Messiah/Jesus)

shall make it
(Jerusalem and the sanctuary/temple)

desolate
(spiritually),

even until the consummation
(end of this time leading up to Jesus' Second Coming/or time of the Gentiles being fulfilled; Luke 21:24),

and that determined
(that which is precisely settled/established)

shall be poured upon the desolate
(shall come upon Jerusalem and the sanctuary/temple).

H) The Parable of the Ten Virgins, told in Matthew chapter 25

In verse one, the ten virgins are all Christians and each has a lamp (i.e., the capability to hold oil and give forth light). More specifically each of these virgins/Christians is the lamp. The oil represents the Holy Spirit and the light they (as the lamp) shine forth is the Light of Christ. They are waiting or going forth to meet their Bridegroom (Jesus) to be married (i.e. to go to the Marriage Supper of the Lamb).

Verses 2-4 says five were wise and took extra oil. These virgins/Christians have the Holy Spirit and continue to have the Holy Spirit. Later, in verse 8 it says the lamps of the foolish five virgins was gone out or was going out (different Bible versions). Therefore, at some time earlier, all of the virgins had some oil (Holy Spirit) in their lamps (themselves)-i.e.: they had all been Christians at one time.

Verse 6 says that at midnight (a dark time, signifying a time of troubles) the call comes forth for the Christians to go out to meet Jesus. This is a CALL TO MARTYRDOM during the great tribulation during a time called "the first reaping" (Rev 14:13-16) as explained below.

> Rev 14:13 ¶ *And I heard a voice from heaven saying unto me, Write, Blessed are the dead which die in the Lord from henceforth: Yea, saith the Spirit, that they may rest from their labours; and their works do follow them.*
> Rev 14:14 *And I looked, and behold a white cloud,* **and upon the cloud one sat like unto the Son of man, having on his head a golden crown,** *and in his hand a sharp sickle.*
> Rev 14:15 *And another angel came out of the temple, crying with a loud voice to him that sat on the cloud, Thrust in thy sickle, and reap: for the time is come for thee to reap; for the harvest of the earth is ripe.*

Rev 14:16 *And he that sat on the cloud thrust in his sickle on the earth; and the earth was reaped.*

Verse 8-10 of Matthew ch 25 shows that the foolish virgins went away from the coming Bridegroom (rejecting the call to martyrdom) intending to return again to Jesus later.

Those that still had the oil (Holy Spirit) in themselves, still shined forth their Light of Christ (having not denied Him). They did not reject the call (call to martyrdom), and went on (becoming martyrs) to the marriage with Jesus (the Bridegroom). As explained in my book, the marriage supper of the Lamb is immediately after the first reaping (a time of great martyrdom) during the great tribulation period. These people go through martyrdom (refusing to go along with the Antichrist and False Prophet) during this time and are in Heaven before the start of the Marriage Supper.

Later, in verses 11-12, those without oil (having lost the Holy Spirit by siding with the Antichrist and False Prophet) seek Jesus later after the start of the Marriage Supper of the Lamb, and the Bridegroom/Jesus says He does not know them (anymore). This is because they have forsaken the Holy Spirit and Jesus.

I) Luke chapter 17 and Matthew chapter 24: one taken the other left

Luke 17:24 *For as the lightning, that lighteneth out of the one part under heaven, shineth unto the other part under heaven; so shall also the Son of man be in his day.*

Luke 17:25 *But first must he suffer many things, and be rejected of this generation.*

Luke 17:26 *And as it was in the days of Noe, so shall it be also in the days of the Son of man.*

Luke 17:27 *They did eat, they drank, they married wives, they were given in marriage, until the day that Noe entered into the ark, and the flood came, and destroyed them all.*

Luke 17:28 *Likewise also as it was in the days of Lot; they did eat, they drank, they bought, they sold, they planted, they builded;*

Luke 17:29 *But the same day that Lot went out of Sodom it rained fire and brimstone from heaven, and destroyed them all.*

Luke 17:30 *Even thus shall it be in the day when the Son of man is revealed.*

Luke 17:31 *In that day, he which shall be upon the housetop, and his stuff in the house, let him not come down to take it away: and he that is in the field, let him likewise not return back.*

Luke 17:32 *Remember Lot's wife.*

Luke 17:33 *Whosoever shall seek to save his life shall lose it; and whosoever shall lose his life shall preserve it.*

Luke 17:34 *I tell you, in that night there shall be two men in one bed; the one shall be taken, and the other shall be left.*

Luke 17:35 *Two women shall be grinding together; the one shall be taken, and the other left.*

Luke 17:36 *Two men shall be in the field; the one shall be taken, and the other left.*

Luke 17:37 *And they answered and said unto him, Where, Lord? And he said unto them, Wheresoever the body is, thither will the eagles be gathered together.*

Mat 24:37 *But as the days of Noe were, so shall also the coming of the Son of man be.*

Mat 24:38 *For as in the days that were before the flood they were eating and drinking, marrying and giving in marriage, until the day that Noe entered into the ark,*

Mat 24:39 *And knew not until the flood came, and took them all away; so shall also the coming of the Son of man be.*

Mat 24:40 *Then shall two be in the field; the one shall be taken, and the other left.*

Mat 24:41 *Two women shall be grinding at the mill; the one shall be taken, and the other left.*

Mat 24:42 *Watch therefore: for ye know not what hour your Lord doth come.*

Mat 24:43 *But know this, that if the goodman of the house had known in what watch the thief would come, he would have watched, and would not have suffered his house to be broken up.*

Mat 24:44 *Therefore be ye also ready: for in such an hour as ye think not the Son of man cometh.*

In Luke 17:24 & 30 it says this is talking about when the Son of Man (Jesus) is REVEALED: I.E.: the Second Coming. This is not talking about a pre-tribulation rapture. In both the times of Noah and Lot, some people are destroyed and some are not destroyed, and so it is here at Jesus' Second Coming also. Also in Luke 17:31, it is talking about a person's choice to flee the area physically, not to be pulled out in a rapture. This verse 31 corresponds to Zech 14:4-5.

Zech 14:4 *And his feet shall stand in that day upon the mount of Olives, which is before Jerusalem on the east, and the mount of Olives shall cleave in the midst thereof toward the east and toward the west, and there shall be a very great valley; and half of the mountain shall remove toward the north, and half of it toward the south.*

Zech 14:5 *And ye shall flee to the valley of the mountains; for the valley of the mountains shall reach unto Azal: yea, ye shall flee, like as ye fled from before the earthquake in the days of Uzziah king of Judah: and the LORD my God shall come, and all the saints with thee.*

Appendix II

Glossary of Terms and Symbols

(From the Book: *Understanding the Book of Revelation*)

Antichrist/Abaddon/Apollyon-Rev 9:11
See Beast (Antichrist)-Rev 13:1-10

Babylon (mighty city)-Rev 18:2&10
The religion and city of the great Whore (the locality in and around Rome; now meaning more specifically the Vatican. See Rev ch 17 notes, especially 17:1, 5 & 18.

Beast (Antichrist)-Rev 13:1-10
It looks like a leopard, but with feet like a bear, and a mouth like a lion. This beast has 7 heads, 10 horns, and 10 crowns. This is the second spirit of the unholy trinity-the Antichrist, which is an evil spirit. This spirit is also Abaddon, also called Apollyon, (Rev 9:11), the king/leader of, and released from, the bottomless pit.

Beast (scarlet)-Rev 17:3, 8, 11; 19:20
With names of blasphemy, having 7 heads and 10 horns. The Antichrist-an evil spirit. Same beast as "Beast (Antichrist)-Rev 13:1-10".

Beast (False Prophet)-Rev 13:11-17
Beast (an evil spirit) spoken of as rising up out of the earth. See "False Prophet-Rev 19:20". He causes people to follow and worship the Antichrist.

Bride (Lamb's wife)-Rev 21:9
Those people who attended the "Marriage Supper of the Lamb (Rev 19:9)".

Dragon/Devil/Satan-Rev 20:3
Satan/fallen Lucifer.

Dragon (great/huge fiery- red (Amplified Bible))- Rev 12:3,9,13-17
Satan/Devil/old serpent. It has 7 heads with 7 crowns. And it has 10 horns, Same as Rev 20:3.

False Prophet-Rev 19:20
Leader of Whore/great whore/apostate church. Story told in Rev 13:11-18 and chapters 17 and 18.

First Resurrection-Rev 20:4&5
Just after Jesus' Second Coming. Comprised of those who will then live and reign with Christ for a thousand years.

Great Supper of God-Rev 19:17
Birds to eat the dead bodies of the ungodly after the battle of Armageddon at Jesus' Second Coming.

Great Tribulation Period-Rev 2:22 & 7:14

Begins with resurrection of the two witness's bodies (Rev 11:11-13) shortly after the Antichrist is in control on Earth (Rev ch 13), includes the time of the great multitude to be clothed in white robe (great tribulation martyrs-Rev 7:9-17), the first reaping" (Rev 14:12-16) to the time the bride of the Lamb has made herself ready (Rev 19:7). It ends before the 7 vials/bowls of Rev chapter 16.

Great White Throne (Judgment Day) Rev 20:11-15

Judgment Day at the end of the world. People not in the First Resurrection are judged. Some inherit eternal life. Some condemned to the lake of fire.

Heads (7)-Rev 17:9&10

Seven mountains and seven kings. The seven mountains are those of Rome, Italy. The seven kings are the sequential kings of the country of Vatican, established in 1929.

Horns (10)-Rev 17:3, 12, 16

10 kings. Receive power as kings one hour with the scarlet beast.

Lamb (of God)-Rev 5:12

Jesus

Man child-Rev 12:5

Jesus

Marriage Supper of the Lamb (Rev 19:9)

For those invited, after the Great Tribulation Period, before Jesus' Second Coming, beginning when nobody else can enter the temple in Heaven (Rev 15:8), and 7 vials/bowls of Gods wrath begin on Earth.

Mystery, Babylon-Rev 17:5

See Whore (great whore)

New Heaven & New Earth-Rev 21:1
Made after Great White Throne Judgment.

Second Death-Rev 20:6, 14, 15
The lake of burning fire.

Unholy Trinity (Rev 16:13, 19:20-20:1, & 20:10)
Satan (the Devil or the Dragon), the beast (the Antichrist), and the False Prophet

Water of Life-Rev 21:6 & 22:1
Holy Spirit (of God)

Wife/Bride (of the Lamb)-Rev 19:7-9
See "Bride (Lamb's wife)-Rev 21:9"

Whore (great whore)-Rev 17:1, 9, 18
The false, apostate religion/church, headquartered in the Vatican. This is now centered adjacent to a city of seven mountains/hills: Rome.

Woman (clothed with sun)-Rev 12:1
God's true Church (OT & NT believers)

Appendix III

ENDNOTES

Endnote 1: Dr. Bill Hamon, *the ETERNAL CHURCH*, (Point Washington, FL; Christian International Publishers, c1981), pp 88-89

Endnote 2: Everett F. Harrison, *Baker's Dictionary of Theology*, (Grand Rapids, Michigan; Baker Book House, c1960), pp. 530

Endnote 3: William Smith, Smith's Bible Dictionary, (Old Tappan, N.J.; SPIRE BOOKS, 15th printing, 1980), pp. 333

Endnote 4: Microsoft Encarta Encyclopedia Standard 2004, © 1993-2003 Microsoft Corporation, articles "Papal States" and "Vatican City"

Endnote 5: Ralph Woodrow, *The Babylon Connection?*, (Palm Springs, CA; Ralph Woodrow Evangelistic Association, Inc, c 1997), second printing, pp 50

Endnote 6: George Eldon Ladd, *A THEOLOGY OF THE NEW TESTAMENT*, (Grand Rapids, MI; William B. Eerdmans Publishing Company, c1974), pp 677-78

Endnote 7: Charles and Frances Hunter, *Angels on Assignment,* (Kingwood, Texas; Hunter Books, c1979), pp. 167

Endnote 8: Matthew Henry, *Matthew Henry's Commentary In One Volume*, (Grand Rapids, MI; Zondervan Publishing House, c 1961) pp. 1102-3

Endnote 9: Compilation from John Foxe and other Eminent Authorities, *Foxe's Christian Martyrs of the World*, (Westwood, New Jersey; Barbour and Company, Inc., c 1985) pp. 231-233

Endnote 10: Charles and Frances Hunter, *Angels on Assignment,* (Kingwood, Texas; Hunter Books, c1979), pp. 87-88

Appendix IV

Bibliography

1. Foxe, John and other Eminent Authorities, *Foxe's Christian Martyr's of the World,* Westwood, New Jersey; Barbour and Company, Inc, c 1985
2. Hammon, Bill, Dr., *the ETERNAL CHURCH,* Point Washington, FL: Christian International Publishers, c1981
3. Harrison, Everett F., *Baker's Dictionary of Theology,* Grand Rapids, MI; Baker Book House, c1960
4. Henry, Matthew, *Matthew Henry's Commentary In One Volume,* Grand Rapids, MI; ZondervanPublishingHouse, c1961
5. Hunter, Charles and Frances (as told by Roland Buck), *Angels on Assignment,* Kingwood, Texas; Hunter Books, c1979
6. Ladd, George Eldon, *A THEOLOGY OF THE NEW TESTAMENT,* Grand Rapids, MI; William B. Eerdmans Publishing Company, c1974
7. Mauro, Philip, *The Seventy Weeks and the Great Tribulation,* available online with the Online Bible at: http://www.onlinebible.net/
8. Microsoft, *Microsoft Encarta Encyclopedia Standard 2004*, c 1993-2003
9. Smith, William, *Smith's Bible Dictionary*, Old Tappan, NJ; SPIRE BOOKS, 15th printing, published1980
10. Strong, James, *The Exhaustive Concordance of the Bible*, Iowa Falls, Iowa; World Bible Publishers. Note: this and an electronic version of this 1890 version and Greek and Hebrew Lexicons for the

Online Bible were used; The Greek lexicon based on Thayer's and Smith's Bible Dictionary plus others; this is keyed to the large Kittel and the "Theological Dictionary of the New Testament." The Hebrew lexicon is Brown, Driver, Briggs, Gesenius Lexicon; this is keyed to the "Theological Word Book of the Old Testament." This electronic combination version is available from http://www.online-bible.com/maconlinebible.html

11. Velez, Thomas, *Understanding the Book of Revelation*; Advantage Books, www.advbooks.com, thomasvelez.com, c2005

12. Woodrow, Ralph, *The Babylon Connection?*, Palm Springs, CA; Ralph Woodrow Evangelistic Association, Inc., c1997

13. Zondervan Corporation and the Lockman Foundation, *The Amplified Bible*, United States of America; Zondervan Publishing House, c 1987

Thomas Velez is available for speaking engagements and personal appearances. For more information contact Thomas at:

Thomas Velez
ADVANTAGE BOOKS™
PO Box 160847
Altamonte Springs, FL 32716

www.thomasvelez.com

To order additional copies of this book or to see a complete list of all **ADVANTAGE BOOKS™** visit our online bookstore at:

www.advbookstore.com

or call our toll free order number at:

1-888-383-3110

Longwood, Florida, USA

"we bring dreams to life"™
www.advbookstore.com

Notes:

Thomas Velez is available for speaking engagements and personal appearances. For more information contact Thomas at:

Thomas Velez
ADVANTAGE BOOKS™
PO Box 160847
Altamonte Springs, FL 32716

www.thomasvelez.com

To order additional copies of this book or to see a complete list of all **ADVANTAGE BOOKS™** visit our online bookstore at:

www.advbookstore.com

or call our toll free order number at:

1-888-383-3110

Longwood, Florida, USA

"we bring dreams to life"™
www.advbookstore.com

Printed in the United States
91493LV00004B/475-522/A